Vocational Education and Guidance of Negroes

Report of a Survey Conducted by the Office of Education

By

AMBROSE CALIVER

Senior Specialist in the Education of Negroes

NEGRO UNIVERSITIES PRESS

WESTPORT, CONNECTICUT

Originally published in 1937
by the U.S. Government Printing Office, Washington, D.C.

Reprinted in 1970 by
Negro Universities Press
A Division of Greenwood Press, Inc.
Westport, Connecticut

Library of Congress Catalogue Card Number 78-82092

SBN 8371-3208-8

Printed in the United States of America

Contents

TABLES

TABLES IN APPENDIX A

FIGURES

FOREWORD

For a number of years the Office of Education has been interested in making a study of occupational opportunities for Negroes with a view to the expansion and improvement of facilities for vocational education and guidance. Plans were being perfected to request funds from the Civil Works Administration in 1934 when the agency was decentralized and funds for Federal projects discontinued. When funds became available under the provisions of the Emergency Relief Appropriation in 1935 for the employment of educational, professional and clerical persons, the Office of Education was authorized to conduct, in addition to four other projects, a survey of opportunities for vocational education and guidance of Negroes.

An advisory committee of 28 persons representing educational, civic, business, and labor organizations gave valuable counsel during the preliminary stages of the study. Individual members and small groups from this committee continued to be of assistance throughout the survey, either through conferences or by correspondence. Invaluable voluntary services were given also by several persons who acted as project managers in certain States. In addition, many public and private agencies and institutions cooperated by lending members of their staffs to act as supervisors or administrators for a period of from 3 to 14 months; and by lending space and equipment for the use of the survey.

The field work was conducted during 1936 by a staff of 500 Negro relief workers who belonged to the "white-collar" class, and most of whom had college training. During the first half of 1937 the data were tabulated, analyzed, and interpreted by a relief and professional staff in the Office of Education.

To all who cooperated with and who worked on the survey, the Office of Education expresses its sincere appreciation for their interest and services.

The depression brought out rather clearly what had been known for some time in a general way by students of the subject, namely, that the important matter of vocational education and guidance had been approached without definite plan or purpose. Increase in scientific discoveries and inventions, the growth of technology, and the social and economic changes that have taken place during the first quarter of the present century have resulted in widespread vocational maladjustments. Occupations have greatly increased in number, specialization, and complication. The demands upon workers have increased and are more exacting. It has become more difficult for one to choose a career, and to prepare for, to enter upon, and to make progress in it. In order to correct these maladjustments a great deal more must be known about future workers and their work. It seemed particularly appropriate, therefore, that relief funds should be used for the prevention of a recurrence of many of these maladjustments.

Because of the narrow economic margin on which they operate, their lack of educational opportunity, and their general social status, the problems mentioned above are particularly acute for Negroes. The situation has been more serious because of a lack of information concerning important phases of the problem. The purpose of this survey is to supply some of the needed information and to assist in pointing the way toward a better adjustment between education and occupational life. This report constitutes what might be termed a statistical source book of basic data resulting from the survey. While it is recognized that it is only a beginning in the solution of a major problem, it is hoped that it will be helpful to schools and other agencies as they endeavor to expand and improve the facilities and opportunities for vocational education and guidance of Negroes.

BESS GOODYKOONTZ,

Assistant Commissioner of Education.

CHAPTER I

Introductory Statement

PEOPLE IN ALL walks of life have found it necessary to make adjustments to new occupational situations resulting from recent developments in science and technology. Although Negroes have shown exceptional capacity in the past to adopt the American social and economic order, they are finding it difficult to adjust themselves to our present modern industrial society. This is not surprising, for adjustments required today are quite different from those required in the past, and are taxing the best thought and energies of the most advanced people.

The problems resulting from this situation have been made especially acute for Negroes. One such problem is the reduction in the number of jobs. As simple manual occupations became mechanized white persons sought the jobs formerly held by Negroes, which, under changed conditions, demanded new skills and knowledge and which paid higher wages. In many cases, Negroes were not prepared to meet the new demands of these jobs, and in other cases they were not employed if white persons were available. In addition to losing jobs formerly held, Negroes have found few opportunities in the new occupations resulting from recent technological progress.

The problem has been accentuated by: (1) lack of education; (2) lack of educational opportunities and adaptation of education to needs; (3) lack of versatility and skill arising from limited occupational experience; and (4) attitude toward work.

Studies [1] have been made in addition to the present survey, which show the following educational conditions among Negroes: (1) A high illiteracy rate; (2) high pupil mortality;[2] (3) large numbers of children who are overage;[2] (4) large numbers of children out of school; (5) poor school attendance; (6) lack of operation of compulsory school attendance laws;

---

[1] Redcay, E. E. County Training Schools and Public Secondary Education for Negroes in the South. Washington, The John F. Slater Fund, 1935.

Blose, David T. *and* Caliver, Ambrose. Statistics of the Education of Negroes. Washington, Government Printing Office, 1936. (United States Department of the Interior, Office of Education, Bulletin 1935, No. 13.) Journal of Negro Education, 1: 2, July 1932.

Caliver, Ambrose. Availability of Education to Negroes in Rural Communities. Washington, Government Printing Office, 1935. (United States Department of the Interior, Office of Education, Bulletin 1935, No. 12.)

[2] See tables 1 and 2 for data from pupils included in this survey.

1

(7) lack of schools; (8) lack of general curriculum and extracurriculum offerings; (9) lack of vocational offerings and guidance; and (10) lack of adequate financial support.

Approximately 55 percent of the total number of Negroes 10 years old and over gainfully employed are engaged in occupations requiring little or no skill. Since these occupations are usually the first to be affected by any economic upheaval and are the most easily dispensed with, Negro unskilled workers are among the first affected during any period of occupational readjustment.

In the South there have been strong traditions with reference to manual labor. The white aristocracy for generations scorned it as beneath their dignity, an attitude which was probably a by-product of the institution of slavery. When Negroes became free, they adopted similar prejudices in their struggle for recognition and self-respect. This attitude frequently prevented them from recognizing the possibilities of improvement in the simple, manual tasks in which the majority of them were engaged.

As a result of such problems the Office of Education became interested, and in 1935 was granted $234,934 through Federal emergency funds to conduct the National Survey of Vocational Education and Guidance of Negroes. The purpose of this survey was to investigate the opportunities and facilities for vocational education and guidance of Negroes in rural and urban communities. The specific objectives were:

1. To analyze the vocational offerings of selected high schools, colleges, evening and proprietary schools, and non-school agencies.
2. To analyze the content and method of teaching these courses in selected institutions.
3. To determine the availability of facilities and equipment for vocational courses.
4. To ascertain the training and qualifications of the teachers of vocational courses.
5. To discover the extent to which organized personnel and guidance services are available to Negro high school and college youth.
6. To study certain characteristics of (1) students enrolled in high schools, colleges, evening and proprietary schools, and non-school agencies, and (2) graduates and non-graduates of high schools, 1926–1935, who had had no further formal education.
7. To ascertain the attitudes of students and educational leaders toward the vocational training of Negroes.

The study was conducted by a director, an associate director, 4 regional directors, 42 State supervisors and project managers, and approximately 500 investigators.[3]

---

[3] See appendix B for fuller statement concerning staff.

SCOPE OF THE STUDY

Within the limit of funds and the designated time, it was not possible to include every high school attended by Negro youth. In view of the fact that the scope of the Survey was national, it was felt that a true picture of the high-school situation could be secured through the selection and study of school administrative units that were typical of the States in those regions in which the majority of the Negro population lives. The States of the northern region are an exception because of the concentration of Negroes in the urban centers. Institutions of higher learning were not selected; all that could be heard from were included in the study.

Selection of units for study of high schools.—With the aid of an advisory committee, directors of Negro education, and regional directors and project supervisors on the staff of the survey, urban and rural centers (approximately 200) in the Southern States were selected on the basis of the characteristics of the Negro population and of their occupations. In these States this selection included most of the larger urban centers and a sufficient number of rural units—counties or parishes—to represent the Negro population as a whole. In the Northern States, where the Negro is an urban dweller, all of the larger cities were included. States having areas included in the study follow:

Alabama.	Kansas.	Ohio.
Arkansas.	Kentucky.	Oklahoma.
California.	Louisiana.	Pennsylvania.
Colorado.	Maryland.	South Carolina.
Connecticut.	Massachusetts.	Tennessee.
Delaware.	Michigan.	Texas.
District of Columbia.	Minnesota.	Virginia.
Florida.	Mississippi.	Washington.
Georgia.	Missouri.	West Virginia.
Illinois.	New Jersey.	Wisconsin.
Indiana.	New York.	
Iowa.	North Carolina.	

The institutions.—The high schools included in the survey comprise the 4-year, and separate junior and senior high schools of each administrative unit. High schools of the northern region which enroll Negro students were included. All colleges for Negroes were included, but only those curriculums directly related to the subject of the survey were studied.

The following institutions of higher education were included:

Benedict College.	Simmons University.
Bennett College.	Howe-Roger-Williams Institute.
Claflin College.	Oakwood College.
Virginia Union University.	LeMoyne College.
Howard University.	Clark University.
Morgan College.	Lane College.
Shaw University.	Miles Memorial College.
St. Paul Normal and Industrial School.	Bishop Tuttle Training School.
Morris Brown College.	Atlanta School for Social Work.
Selma University.	Prairie View State College.

Oklahoma C. A. & N. University.	Arkansas A. & M. College.
North Carolina N. A. & T. College.	Houston College for Negroes.
Princess Anne Academy.	Lincoln University (Mo.).
Alcorn A. & M. College.	Southern University.
Virginia State College.	Delaware State College.
Alabama State A. & M. College.	Kentucky State Industrial College.
West Virginia State College.	Louisville Municipal College.
Florida A. & M. College.	North Carolina College for Negroes.
Hampton Institute.	Winston-Salem Teachers College.
Tennessee State A. & I. College.	South Carolina State College.
Louisiana Normal and Industrial Institute.	Cheyney Training School for Teachers.
	Tuskegee Institute.

All evening schools, proprietary schools,[4] and nonschool agencies which offer courses in vocational education and guidance for Negroes within the areas studied and from which data could be obtained were included.

DATA AND SOURCES

Enumeration of sources.—Data for the Survey were obtained from the following sources: (1) High schools, (2) colleges, (3) social agencies—such as Y. M. C. A.'s, Y. W. C. A.'s, and community centers, (4) public evening schools, (5) proprietary schools—such as commercial schools and schools of beauty culture, (6) high-school and college teachers, (7) high-school pupils, (8) students in nurse-training institutions, (9) medical schools, (10) graduates and former students of high schools, (11) evening school students, (12) Statistical Division of the Office of Education, and (13) the Vocational Education Division of the Office of Education.[5]

Inquiry forms.—Most of the data were collected on inquiry forms. Fourteen forms, which are described in appendix B, were used for this purpose.

Other sources of data.—Data concerning the enrollments, courses, teachers, and expenditures in schools having federally aided vocational education programs were tabulated directly from the State reports filed in the Vocational Education Division of the Office of Education. A study was made of the trends in these items from 1928–29 to 1934–35, inclusive.

Letters were sent to a number of educators and employment executives in order to ascertain their views and suggested solutions relative to the special problems in vocational education and occupational adjustment of Negroes.

With two exceptions, all data were gathered by personal contact and interview by qualified persons, working under the immediate direction of a local supervisor, and the general direction of a State supervisor. The two exceptions referred to were data collected on forms mailed directly to the institutions concerned.

Accuracy and reliability of data.—It is believed that the use of the inquiry forms through the interview method assured a high degree of accuracy and

---

[4] Private schools operated by a proprietor, such as certain commercial schools, schools of beauty culture, etc.
[5] All data on the federally aided vocational education program in this study are from the 18 States maintaining separate schools for the Negro and white races.

reliability. Moreover, an additional precaution was taken by having the local supervisor check each form. The supervisors were selected for their superior ability and acquaintance with the schools and local community in general. Samplings of these forms were checked by the State supervisor and the regional director.

Cooperation of school officials and other citizens.—An investigation of such wide scope as this could not be possible but for the generous cooperation of many individuals and organizations. Letters from the Assistant Commissioner of Education were sent to State superintendents of education requesting their cooperation in making the survey. Similar letters were sent to State directors of Negro education and to the superintendent of each rural and urban administrative unit from which data were gathered. Prior to visits to institutions by members of the staff, a letter requesting cooperation was sent to its executive head from the Director of the Survey.

The National Technical Advisory Committee, composed of national leaders in business, industry, and the professions rendered valuable assistance in clarifying the purposes of the survey and in the selection of units for study.

TABLE 1.—*Number and percent of Negro pupils who plan to drop out of high school for the reasons indicated*

Reason	Southwest Number	Southwest Percent	South Atlantic Number	South Atlantic Percent	South Central Number	South Central Percent	Northern Number	Northern Percent	Total Number	Total Percent
1	2	3	4	5	6	7	8	9	10	11
Failure in school work	38	5.7	55	10.0	28	5.9	124	13.0	245	2.1
Lack of interest in school work	15	2.2	13	2.4	14	2.9	63	6.6	105	.9
Lack of relation between school work and anticipated job	20	2.9	10	1.8	7	1.5	23	2.4	60	.5
Opportunity for good job	68	10.2	54	9.8	45	9.6	173	18.1	340	2.9
Desire to earn money for self	152	22.7	109	19.9	171	36.3	212	22.3	644	5.5
To help support family	190	28.5	117	21.3	79	16.8	270	28.3	656	5.5
Poor health	167	25.0	92	16.8	80	17.0	54	5.7	393	3.3
Other	17	2.5	99	18.0	46	9.8	34	3.6	196	1.6
No reason given	2,601	79.6	755	57.9	1,926	80.4	3,999	80.7	9,281	77.9
Total number planning to drop out	3,268		1,304		2,396		4,952		11,920	
Total number planning to drop out giving reasons	667		549		470		953		2,639	
Percentage	20.4		42.1		19.6		19.2		22.1	

TABLE 2.—*Number and percent of Negro high-school pupils who are overage in the grades indicated, according to geographical regions*

Region	GRADE										Grand total	Per-cent
	Eighth¹		Ninth		Tenth		Eleventh		Twelfth			
	Number	Per-cent	Number	Per-cent	Number	Per-cent	Number	Per-cent	Number	Per-cent		
1	2	3	4	5	6	7	8	9	10	11	12	13
Northern	81	61.8	1,144	33.2	777	26.4	627	27.4	352	23.9	2,981	29.0
South Atlantic	628	48.6	625	30.4	457	25.9	413	28.7	108	18.4	2,231	31.2
South Central	153	42.9	495	36.3	380	33.3	280	26.5	238	30.1	1,546	32.9
Southwest	465	51.6	642	42.8	450	36.7	457	37.0	116	30.2	2,130	40.6
Total overage	1,327	49.5	2,906	34.8	2,064	29.2	1,777	29.5	814	25.2	8,888	32.5
Total in grade	2,681	----	8,362	----	7,073	----	6,014	----	3,236	----	27,366	----

¹ In several States in the South where the elementary schools consist of 7 grades, the eighth grade constitutes the first year of high school.

CHAPTER II

Summary of Findings, Conclusions, and Recommendations

FINDINGS

SCHOOLS AND COLLEGES

General.—

1. The total number of vocational courses offered in the 207 high schools studied increased from 1930 to 1935; the largest increases were in home economics, industrial arts, and agriculture; the largest decreases were in the building trades.
2. Slight increases were found in the number of courses offered in radio repairing, aviation, refrigeration, janitorial work, beauty culture, cafeteria management, and vocational guidance.
3. Nearly half (46.4 percent) of the pupils in the high schools studied were registered in academic curriculums in 1934–35.
4. Public colleges studied offer more courses in home economics and agriculture than in any other vocational subject.
5. Fewer colleges than high schools reported changes in the number of vocational courses offered from 1930 to 1935.
6. Fewer college students registered for vocational courses in 1934–35 than in 1930–31, though the percentage of such students to the total enrollment increased.
7. In each State studied, except one, the percentage of all Federal funds for vocational education spent on high-school courses for Negroes was lower than the percentage of Negroes to the total population.
8. The number of vocational courses offered, teachers employed, pupils enrolled, and the expenditures for vocational courses among Negroes increased between 1928–29 and 1934–35.
9. There were in 1935–36, 1,726 rural schools for Negroes offering 1 or more years of high-school instruction.

Courses in agriculture.—

1. In 1934–35, 542 all-day high schools for Negroes, 320 part-time schools, and 784 evening schools, participated in the Federal program of vocational education in agriculture. Most of these schools are operated in the same building and are taught by the same teachers.

8

2. From 1926–27 to 1934–35 the percentage of increase in the number of all-day schools for Negroes offering vocational agriculture was 73.7. In number of evening, part-time, and day unit classes, the percentage increase from 1928–29 to 1934–35 was 128.7.
3. The percentages of Negro males enrolled in each type of federally aided schools offering courses in vocational agriculture of the total Negroes enrolled are: For 1928–29: All-day, 52.4; evening, 29.9; part-time, 7.9; day unit, 9.7. For 1934–35: All-day, 38.8; evening, 40.2; part-time 10.2; day unit, 10.6.
4. The percentage increases of enrollment of Negroes in all types of federally aided schools offering courses in vocational agriculture in 1934–35 over 1928–29 were: Males, 110.9; females, 273.1; in all-day schools the corresponding percentage increases were for males, 111, and for females, 122.
5. The three major occupations for which the land-grant colleges for Negroes prepared their graduates of agricultural courses in 1934–35 were: (1) Teaching vocational subjects in high school; (2) extension work; and (3) college teaching. In 1935–36, the percentages of the total Negro and total white graduates in the South trained as teachers of vocational agriculture were, respectively, 91.6 and 41.2.
6. The number of Negro teachers of agriculture in all-day schools increased 35 percent from 1928–29 to 1934–35; the number of persons enrolled in courses for the training of teachers of agriculture increased 6.5 percent during the same period.
7. Of all Federal funds allotted to the preparation of teachers of agriculture in the 18 States studied, the proportion allotted to courses for Negroes ranged from 11.1 to 16.1 percent during the period 1928–29 to 1934–35.
8. Of the Federal funds allotted to instruction in agriculture in the 18 States studied, the proportion allotted to courses for Negroes ranged from 8 percent in 1928–29 to 12 percent in 1934–35.

Courses in home economics.—
1. There were 225 all-day schools for Negroes in the 18 States studied offering federally aided vocational courses in home economics in 1934–35; an increase of 543 percent since 1928–29.
2. In 1934–35, 508 classes were offered Negroes in vocational home economics in evening schools; or 316 percent increase over 1928–29.
3. In the 207 selected high schools, in 1934–35, 14 percent of the girls were enrolled in home economics curriculums. In the schools for Negroes which made the regular statistical report to the Office of Education for 1934, 21.8 percent of the girls were enrolled in general home economics in the 4-year high schools and 18.8 percent in the junior-senior high schools.

4. The enrollment of Negro girls in federally aided home economics courses increased 195.3 percent from 1928–29 to 1934–35.
5. Four percent of the Negro girls 15 to 19 years of age in the 18 States studied were enrolled in federally aided home economics courses in all-day schools in 1934–35.
6. Few Negro girls are enrolled in federally aided part-time home economics courses.
7. From 1928–29 to 1934–35 the number of Negro home economics teachers in federally aided all-day schools increased from 50 to 231, or 362 percent; those in evening schools from 136 to 276, or 103 percent.
8. The percentage of Federal funds received for vocational home economics in all types of schools for Negroes ranged from 8.2 to 10.2 for the 7 years, 1928 to 1935.

Courses in trades and industries.—
1. There were 61 all-day schools offering federally aided vocational courses in trades and industries for Negroes in 1934–35, or an increase of 52.5 percent over 1928–29.
2. In 1934–35 Negro pupils in federally aided all-day schools were registered in 13 different trades and industries courses; in evening schools, 14; and in part-time and trade extension courses, 8.
3. Few Negro students, enrolled in the high schools reporting to the Office of Education, or in the 10 public colleges studied, were registered in trade and industrial courses.
4. The number of Negro boys and men enrolled in federally aided vocational courses in trades and industries in 18 States increased from 4,232 in 1928–29 to 6,324 in 1934–35, or 49 percent; girls and women, from 2,286 in 1928–29 to 3,255 in 1934–35, or 42.3 percent.
5. The number of Negro teachers of federally aided trades and industries courses in federally aided all-day schools increased from 87 in 1928–29 to 144 in 1934–35, or 40 percent; in evening schools, 130 to 254, or 95 percent; in part-time trade extension schools, 14 to 58, or 314 percent. The number of teachers in the part-time general continuation schools decreased from 23 to 13, or 77 percent.
6. The percentage of expenditures of Federal funds for trades and industries allotted to schools for Negroes ranged from 4.4 to 6.7 during the 7 years studied.

TEACHERS AND TEACHING

Teachers.—
1. The typical vocational teacher of Negroes is a college graduate. The difference in training of such teachers among the sections of the country is slight.

2. Home economics teachers have more specialized training than teachers of the other vocational subjects. The median number of semester hours credit for teachers of home economics is 38.89; for teachers of commerce, 27.43; for teachers of agriculture, 30; for teachers of theory, 30.14; and for teachers of trades and industries, 30.81.

3. Most of the vocational teachers studied have remained in their positions from 6 to 10 years, and half of them have had 6 or more years of experience in occupations related to their fields of teaching.

4. The median age of the vocational teachers studied is 37.3 years.

5. The median annual salary of the vocational teachers studied is $1,871.74. The salaries of teachers of the different vocational subjects vary only slightly from this median with the exception of teachers of agriculture, for whom the median salary is $1,060 There is a marked difference in median annual salary of teachers among the different States.

6. From 1928–29 to 1934–35 the percentage increases in the enrollment of Negroes in teacher-training classes were as follows for the different subjects: Agriculture (men), 6.6; trades and industries (men), 80, (women) 54.8 for 1933–34; [1] and home economics (women), 58.7.

Teaching.—

1. Most of the vocational courses taught by the teachers responding are 1 year in length and are offered each year. Few courses were offered in alternate years.

2. A large percentage of the teachers offer vocational or prevocational courses in the seventh and eighth grades.

3. Most of the teachers devote three-fourths of the class time to laboratory or shop work and one-fourth to group discussion and theory.

4. "Quality of product" was the most frequently mentioned criterion used for determining students' marks.

HIGH-SCHOOL PUPILS, GRADUATES AND NONGRADUATES

High-school pupils.—

1. The occupational status of fathers of children studied seems to influence the educational level attained by the children.

2. The typical parent of the pupils studied had reached the eighth grade.

3. Thirty-six percent of the parents own their homes. The median number of books in each home is 60. Eighty-five percent subscribe to a daily paper, and 70 percent subscribe to a Negro weekly paper.

4. A large number of the pupils supported themselves wholly or in part while in school; 17 percent, wholly; and 47 percent, in part.

5. One-third of the 27,366 pupils studied are overage for their grade.

---

[1] Data not given for 1934–35.

6. Occupational choices of Negro pupils studied are limited in range and vary among the geographical regions and communities of different sizes, but not according to age or grade level of pupil, and only slightly according to fathers' occupation, or parents' education.

7. "Desire to make money" and "belief in their ability" were the two strongest influences which pupils said affected selection of an occupation. "Desire to serve" was next.

High-school graduates and nongraduates.—

1. In the different geographic regions the median age of male high-school graduates and nongraduates at the time of leaving school ranged, respectively, from 18.7 to 19.4 and from 17.6 to 18.2; females, from 18.4 to 18.9 and 17.3 to 17.8 The median age at the time interviewed (1936) of male and female graduates and nongraduates, respectively, were: Graduates, 23.2 and 22.8; nongraduates 21.9 and 21.8. The median age of those attending evening school is 26 years.

2. Nongraduates and evening school students in the Southern region had approximately a year less of schooling than those in the other regions.

3. A larger percentage of the graduates and nongraduates in the Southern regions than in the Northern and Western pursued academic curriculums while in high school.

4. A larger proportion of the graduates and nongraduates in the Northern regions than in the Southern regions had vocational training while in high school.

5. More persons who received their vocational training in small communities than in the larger ones said that it assisted in obtaining work.

6. Fifty-six percent of the graduates and 44 percent of the nongraduates supported themselves during high-school attendance.

7. The three main reasons the nongraduates studied left high school before graduation are: (*a*) Financial needs of family, (*b*) desire to make money, and (*c*) lack of interest.

8. A larger percentage of the males in the Southern than in the Northern regions went directly to work after leaving school.

9. Most of the persons studied who attend evening schools do so for the purpose of preparing themselves for a new type of work, or in order to improve their chances for an increase in rank or salary.

10. At time of study, the percentages of male graduates and nongraduates, respectively, who had never been employed were 6.9 and 8.3; female graduates and nongraduates, 21.7 and 28.5.

11. Most of the graduates and nongraduates studied obtained their jobs through friends or relatives, or by direct application. Few said that the school had assisted them.

12. Evening school students who received aid in obtaining their first job from teachers or the placement bureau of the school had attended school longer than the others. Those who obtained their first job through former students had attended school less than the others.

GUIDANCE

1. Few institutions for Negroes have organized guidance programs.
2. A variety of organizations and officers are responsible for guidance in the institutions that provide it.
3. A larger number of institutions obtain information about the "family status" of pupils and students than about any other background factor studied.
4. The largest number of schools and colleges obtain information about pupils and students through "conferences."
5. Exploratory courses are offered by about one-third of the schools reporting.
6. "Lectures and assembly programs" were the procedure used by most of the institutions in giving the student information about occupations. Six high schools and no colleges used "contacts with industrial, trade, and commercial establishments." Four schools and two colleges used "occupational surveys."
7. While half of the institutions replying kept "cumulative record cards," few institutions use the data recorded for guidance purposes.
8. Two-thirds of the high schools and practically all the colleges replying reported some type of placement and follow-up service.
9. Objectives of the guidance program vary greatly among the institutions replying.

CONCLUSIONS

1. Improvement in the education of Negroes for effective occupational adjustment is largely dependent on improvement of general education. For example, there should be reduction of illiteracy, increase in school facilities, increase in the ability of schools to hold pupils, reduction of the number of pupils over-age for their grades, and an enrichment of the curriculum and extracurriculum offerings.
2. The adequacy of the program of vocational instruction for Negroes varies among the different fields studied. More or less improvement in each field is needed: (1) In the number of schools offering and in facilities for vocational instruction; (2) in number of courses adapted to modern occupational demands; (3) in number of students enrolled in many courses now offered; (4) in number and quality of preparation of vocational teachers; and (5) in financial support.
3. Guidance programs for Negroes are inadequate in number and quality. Improvement is needed with respect to: (1) Organization and administration; (2) information obtained about students and occupations; (3) use of information obtained; and (4) guidance services.

4. The curriculum and occupational choice of Negro students indicate a limited educational and vocational outlook.

RECOMMENDATIONS

In view of the findings and conclusions resulting from this survey, the following recommendations are made:

1. That the land-grant colleges in each State, particularly those for Negroes, since in many States they are the only publicly controlled institutions of higher learning which they may attend, (1) make special studies of problems concerned with the future vocational success of Negroes, especially within the areas they serve; (2) participate actively in the State educational program looking toward the solution of these problems; (3) cooperate with all possible agencies, such as the colleges and universities, extension workers, industrial and business leaders, agricultural employers, and interested public officials and lay citizens, in improving the employment status of and educational facilities for Negroes; (4) cooperate with other land-grant colleges for Negroes within a given region, through conferences and otherwise, in the study of problems common to the particular area; (5) encourage more of their students to consider the vocational needs of Negroes and to pursue courses other than those leading to teaching.

2. That the Negro citizens, in cooperation with the faculties of the land-grant college, vocational teacher-trainers and supervisors, farm and home demonstration agents, and Jeanes teachers, make a study of the needs of Negroes for vocational education and present their findings to the school officials. Such a group should acquaint itself with the provisions of the Federal aid program for vocational education, and through the local school officials seek to share in its benefits.

3. That the group give consideration also to the improvement of the general educational situation among Negroes with respect to (1) establishing needed and accessible high schools; (2) increasing facilities for vocational instruction; (3) enforcing school attendance laws; (4) encouraging an increase in the number, qualification, and compensation of teachers and supervisors.

4. That schools for Negroes give more attention to ways and means of (1) providing courses, as rapidly as means and personnel permit, that will meet the needs and interests of students and the growing occupational demands; (2) reducing pupil mortality; (3) adapting materials and methods of teaching to the needs of modern occupational life.

5. That, as rapidly as possible, schools for Negroes institute a definite program of guidance in charge of qualified persons, beginning with the junior high school grades and continuing through college, which should include: (1) the application of modern techniques for the study of individual interests, needs, and aptitudes; (2) frequent studies of the occupations and the status and trend of Negro employment in the community, State, and Nation; (3) student counseling based on approved procedures; and (4) counseling adults employed and those unemployed.

6. That extension education be established where necessary by schools and available colleges for the purpose of (1) providing reeducation to youth and adults; (2) assisting both in keeping abreast of the changing occupational demands; and (3) repairing the defects resulting from inadequate earlier education.

7. That schools cooperate with interested individuals and groups in making contacts with employers for the purpose of opening up more occupational opportunities for Negroes and of assisting them to enter the new fields that are being developed.

8. That schools endeavor to change the attitude of Negroes toward occupations and the training opportunities designed to assist them to improve in and to retain the jobs they now have, and to prepare them for new opportunities as they become available.

9. That individuals and groups interested in the improvement of educational facilities for Negroes continue and increase their efforts to promote equitability of educational opportunity and equitability in the distribution of funds without regard to race or color, especially with respect to Federal and State funds allotted to education.

═══[*CHAPTER III*]═══

The General Educational Program and
The Place of Vocational Training

G UIDANCE in the selection of vocations and preparation for effective participation in them are two of the major functions of education. Because of the demands of modern society, more attention is now given to these functions than ever before. If one is to obtain a clear picture of this phase of education for Negroes, it is necessary to study its setting in the general education program. Heretofore, detailed skills and knowledge have been stressed in vocational training. At present, specialized skills and related knowledge quickly become outmoded. Educators are beginning to realize that attitudes, perseverance, creative imagination, and certain other personality traits, which should be products of general education, are essential to vocational success. In light of this fact, a study of the status of general education among Negroes is important in revealing the situation in vocational education and guidance, and in suggesting the possibilities for the immediate future. This section is devoted chiefly to a brief discussion of secondary education among Negroes because it is at this level that most of the vocational training programs are found, and with which this survey particularly concerns itself.

Number and distribution of high schools.—While it is difficult to state the exact number of high schools open at any given time, the following data are based on the best available information. In 1936 there were 2,460 schools designated as separate schools for colored children doing 1 or more years of high-school work. Of this number 2,352 were public schools and 108 were private schools. The distribution of these schools among States is shown in table 3. There was an increase of approximately 100 percent in the number of high schools for Negroes since 1930.[1] No attempt was made to classify these schools according to years of work offered, but if the same proportions exist as in 1930, the following classification prevails: 1 year, 17.4 percent; 2 years, 23.6 percent; 3 years, 14.9 percent; 4 years, 44 percent. Rural schools constitute 70 percent of the total.

---

[1] Secondary Education for Negroes. Washington, Government Printing Office, 1933. (United States Department of the Interior, Office of Education. Bulletin 1932, No. 17, Monograph No. 7.)

16

TABLE 3.—*Number and distribution of separate high schools for Negroes*

State	Urban	Rural [1]	Total	Public	Private	Total
1	2	3	4	5	6	7
Alabama	41	223	264	254	10	264
Arkansas	40	111	151	145	6	151
Delaware	1	6	7	7		7
District of Columbia	9		9	9		9
Florida	26	34	60	60		60
Georgia	73	203	276	258	18	276
Illinois	10	4	14	14		14
Indiana	17	11	28	28		28
Kansas	4		4	4		4
Kentucky	44	35	79	78	1	79
Louisiana	26	57	83	72	11	83
Maryland	6	27	33	33		33
Mississippi	96	58	154	129	25	154
Missouri	26	31	57	57		57
New Jersey	1	1	2	1	1	2
North Carolina	64	140	204	196	8	204
Oklahoma	41	43	84	84		84
South Carolina	51	188	239	230	9	239
Tennessee	28	59	87	83	4	87
Texas	86	381	467	461	6	467
Virginia	29	85	114	105	9	114
West Virginia	15	29	44	44		44
Total	734	1,726	2,460	2,352	108	2,460

[1] All schools in communities with a population of less than 5,000 were considered as rural schools.

Availability of high schools.—Several situations must be taken into consideration when discussing the availability of schools. One is the relationship between the number of schools and the number of children of high-school age in the State to be served. This relationship may be observed by comparing data in table 3 with those in table 4. This is a rather coarse measure of availability; a finer one would be a study of the number of schools within a county in relation to the number of children of high-school age in that county. Data were not obtained on this item, but according to the survey on secondary education made in 1930 [2] there was a serious dearth of high schools for Negroes at that time. For example, there were 196 counties having a large Negro population without any 4-year high schools, and 230 such counties with no high-school facilities. Although the number of high schools has increased, facilities are still inadequate. In treating this subject, only those States maintaining separate schools for Negro and white children will be considered.[3]

Where only a few schools are provided for a large area it is inevitable that some are located long distances from the homes of the children. This was found to be the case in the 1930 Survey,[4] and in a later study of the situation in rural areas [5] in 1935.

[2] Ibid., p. 28–29.
[3] In Indiana, New Jersey, and Ohio separate schools are not required by State statute. It is assumed, therefore, that where no separate school exists Negroes attend school with the other children.
[4] Secondary Education for Negroes. Op. cit.
[5] Availability of Education to Negroes in Rural Communities. Op. cit.

TABLE 4.—*Negro high-school population and school enrollment, according to States* [1]

State	Population 15 to 19 years of age	High-school enrollment		
		Number	Percent of Negro population 15 to 19 years of age	Percent of total school enrollment
1	2	3	4	5
Alabama	109, 216	9, 162	8. 4	4. 3
Arkansas	52, 545	4, 038	7. 7	3. 7
Delaware	2, 985	771	25. 8	10. 8
District of Columbia	10, 675	5, 382	50. 4	16. 5
Florida	43, 355	5, 550	12. 8	5. 3
Georgia	134, 216	10, 927	8. 1	3. 9
Kentucky	20, 762	7, 079	34. 1	14. 1
Louisiana	81, 293	8, 832	10. 9	5. 3
Maryland	25, 417	5, 536	21. 8	9. 8
Mississippi	114, 893	6, 757	5. 9	2. 3
Missouri	17, 735	6, 033	34. 0	13. 6
North Carolina	115, 166	24, 725	21. 5	8. 8
Oklahoma	18, 811	5, 493	29. 2	11. 5
South Carolina	106, 429	10, 377	9. 7	4. 5
Tennessee	51, 835	10, 751	20. 7	9. 3
Texas	92, 505	25, 505	27. 5	11. 9
Virginia	73, 443	12, 475	16. 9	7. 7
West Virginia	10, 109	3, 792	37. 5	14. 9
Total	1, 081, 581	163, 185	15. 1	6. 7

[1] Original data taken from Statistics of State School Systems, 1933–34, Washington, Government Printing Office, 1936. (United States Department of the Interior, Office of Education, Bulletin 1935, No. 2.)

In the former study it was found that 30 percent of the schools served an area of 30 square miles, while 23 percent served an area of 5 square miles. The significance of these facts can be appreciated when it is realized that transportation facilities provided for Negro children are very inadequate. For example, of 47,073 children replying in the study [6] previously referred to, it was found that only 2,109, or 4.5 percent, were transported to and from school at public expense.

High-school enrollment.—It is difficult to ascertain the exact number of Negro children enrolled in high school. The statistics in the Office of Education are obtained from two sources: (1) From State departments of education; and (2) from schools. In 18 States separate schools are maintained by law for Negro children, in a few other States separate schools have been established in certain communities. In States where Negro children attend school with white children it is frequently not possible to obtain statistics separated by race.

The latest facts available are for the year 1933–34. At that time 163,185 [7] pupils were enrolled in the high schools of the 18 States maintaining separate schools for Negro and white children. Taking the country as a whole the following enrollments of Negro pupils were reported to the Office

[6] Ibid., p. 23.
[7] Statistics of State school systems. *In* Biennial survey of eduation in the United States, 1930–32. Washington, Government Printing Office, 1935. (United States Department of the Interior, Office of Education, Bulletin 1935, No. 2.) p. 96.

of Education by the different kinds of secondary schools for the year 1933–34: Regular high schools, 130,478; senior high schools, 15,104; junior-senior high schools, 15,569; and junior high schools, 44,035. This gives a total of 205,186 Negro pupils enrolled in schools organized to do secondary work,[8] including the junior high schools.

The Negro population 15–19 years of age, inclusive, in the 18 States maintaining separate schools is 1,081,581. Fifteen percent of this number is enrolled in high school. The percentages of Negro children 15–19 years of age enrolled in the last 4 years of high school in the 15 States studied increased from 9.5 in 1930 to 14.3 in 1934.

Attendance at reorganized schools.—Among some of the features of reorganized schools,[9] the following appear to have important implications for vocational education and guidance: (1) Greater provision for articulation between the upper high-school unit and the preceding school unit; (2) more systematic educational and vocational guidance; (3) greater flexibility and comprehensiveness of the program of studies; and (4) more attention to and development of extracurriculum activities. In view of these advantages it should be of interest to inquire into the extent to which Negroes have attended junior high schools. The number and percentage of pupils reported in this study who attended junior high school for a given period in the different regions are given in table 5 showing that 44.6 percent attended junior high school 1 or more years. This is in close agreement with the findings of the Office of Education in 1934,[10] showing that 47 percent of the pupils in the high schools reporting were enrolled in reorganized schools. There is considerable variation among the different regions in the percentages of Negro pupils attending junior high school; they are, for the respective regions: Southwest, 27.8; South Atlantic, 37.7; South Central, 47; and Northern, 56.8.

TABLE 5.—*Number and percent of pupils who attended and who did not attend junior high school*

1	Southwest		South Atlantic		South Central		Northern		Total	
	Number	Percent	Number	Percent	Number	Percent	Number	Percent	Number	Percent
1	2	3	4	5	6	7	8	9	10	11
Attended junior high school:										
1 year	253	4.8	421	5.6	449	9.4	1,336	12.7	2,459	8.8
2 years	767	14.5	967	12.9	795	16.7	1,912	18.2	4,441	15.8
3 years	450	8.5	1,431	19.2	1,001	20.9	2,717	25.9	5,599	20.0
Did not attend	3,608	68.2	4,029	54.0	2,367	49.7	3,735	35.6	13,739	49.1
No response	215	4.0	607	8.1	153	3.2	788	7.5	1,763	6.3
Total	5,293	------	7,455	------	4,765	------	10,488	------	28,001	------

[8] Statistics of public high schools. *In* Biennial survey of education in the United States, 1930–32. Washington, Government Printing Office, 1935. (United States Department of the Interior, Office of Education, Bulletin 1935, No. 2.) p. 23.
[9] The Reorganization of Secondary Education. Washington, Government Printing Office, 1933. (United State Department of the Interior, Office of Education. Bulletin 1932, No. 17, Monograph No. 5) p. 83.
[10] Statistics of public high schools. Op cit., p. 23.

The lack of high schools for Negroes and the small enrollment in the schools provided, discussed in the preceding sections, have important implications for vocational education and guidance; for, unless there are schools within the reach of children, which they attend, there is little possibility of securing the guidance and training necessary for effective participation in occupational life.

GENERAL SITUATION

Trends in vocational courses in high school.—In order to ascertain trends in high schools, inquiry was made concerning the number of vocational courses added and dropped during the 6-year period between 1930 and 1935. The results of this inquiry are shown in tables 6 and 7.

Number of schools reporting courses added and dropped are shown in table 7. A total of 37 different courses were added. The largest number of additions occurred in home economics, agriculture, and industrial arts, the respective number of schools adding them being 20, 17, and 13. A total of 16 different courses were dropped; those dropped by the largest number of schools were commerce and the building trades; the respective number of schools dropping them being 13 and 6. The specific comparisons between academic and vocational courses were not made in this study, but during the depression certain unpublished studies were made which showed that vocational courses frequently were the first to be dropped when retrenchment became necessary.

While the numbers involved in table 7 are perhaps too small to support definite conclusions, certain facts relative to courses in trades and industries may have some significance. For example, in the building trades and in plumbing the number of courses dropped exceed those added. Another significant fact to which attention should be directed, is the small number of courses added in certain fields in which expansion has taken place. Some of these fields are: Radio repairing, vocational guidance, beauty culture, cafeteria management, and janitorial engineering. In view of the growth in these occupations it would seem advisable for schools to increase the offerings in them.

TABLE 6.—*Number of vocational courses added and dropped by 207 high schools by years from 1930 to 1935*

Year	Courses added	Courses dropped	Year	Courses added	Courses dropped
1930..............	12	8	1934..............	36	7
1931..............	30	3	1935..............	37	4
1932.............	10	14			
1933..............	18	14	Total........	143	50

TABLE 7.—*Number of specified vocational courses added and dropped by 207 high schools for Negroes from 1930 to 1935*

Course	Number of schools adding courses	Number of schools dropping courses	Course	Number of schools adding courses	Number of schools dropping courses
1	2	3	1	2	3
Art appreciation	1		Laundering	1	
Auto mechanics	5	3	Machine shop	1	
Beauty culture	6		Mechanical drawing	3	2
Bookkeeping	2	1	Metal work	2	
Brick masonry	6	3	Millinery		2
Building trades	2	6	Nursing	1	1
Business administration	2		Music	1	1
Cafeteria management	1		Plastering	1	
Carpentry and cabinet making	10	3	Plumbing		3
Commerce	13	13	Printing and duplicating	3	1
Commercial art	4		Salesmanship	2	
Dressmaking	1		Shoe repairing	2	
Electricity	6		Tailoring	3	1
Farm mechanics	2		Teacher training		2
Home economics	20	3	Trade mathematics	1	
Housemaid training	4		Radio repairing	2	
Industrial art	13		Vocational agriculture	17	5
Janitorial engineering	1		Vocational guidance	4	

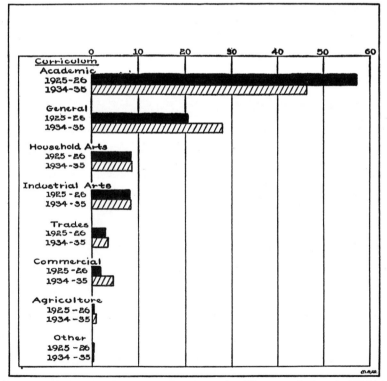

FIGURE 1.—Percentage of Negro pupils registered in different curriculums in 207 high schools, 1925–26 and 1934–35.

Curriculum registrations in high school.—Curriculum registrations in 207 high schools for each year from 1925–26 to 1934–35 are shown in table 8 and figure 1. There were slight changes during the 10-year period in the percentage of the total number of pupils who were registered in agriculture, trades, home economics, and industrial arts. The comparative percentages for the different curriculums are shown below:

Curriculum	1925–26	1934–35
Agriculture	0. 6	0. 9
Trades	2. 9	3. 3
Household arts	8. 3	8. 4
Industrial arts	8. 1	8. 2

There was a decrease in registrations in academic or college-preparatory curriculums from 57.1 percent in 1925–26 to 46.4 percent in 1934–35. While this represents a difference of 10.7 percent, there was an increase in the number of pupils registered in this curriculum of 127 percent. There was an increase in the percentage distribution in the "general curriculum" registrations from 20.5 in 1925 to 27.9 in 1935, and an increase in numbers registered in this curriculum during the same period of 282 percent.

TABLE 8.—*Curriculum registrations for the past 10 years in 207 high schools for Negroes, by sex*

Curriculum	1925-26 Male	Female	Total	1926-27 Male	Female	Total	1927-28 Male	Female	Total	1928-29 Male	Female	Total	1929-30 Male	Female	Total
	2	3	4	5	6	7	8	9	10	11	12	13	14	15	16
Academic or college preparatory:[1] Number	7,669	12,082	20,425	9,185	13,904	23,802	9,963	15,558	26,286	10,247	15,967	26,805	11,104	16,935	28,543
Percent	57.6	55.4	57.1	57.0	57.0	57.8	53.5	54.8	55.0	51.3	51.8	52.7	50.5	51.1	51.7
Agriculture: Number	148	58	206	198	98	296	278	93	371	304	74	378	311	73	384
Percent	1.1	.3	.6	1.2	.4	.7	1.5	.3	.8	1.5	.2	.7	1.4	.2	.7
Commercial: Number	193	506	699	246	461	707	247	529	776	339	764	1,103	444	961	1,405
Percent	1.5	2.3	1.9	1.5	1.9	1.7	1.3	1.8	1.6	1.7	2.5	2.2	2.0	2.9	2.6
Trades: Number	585	485	1,070	688	511	1,199	866	524	1,390	926	478	1,404	1,178	667	1,845
Percent	4.3	2.2	2.9	4.2	2.1	2.9	4.7	1.8	2.9	4.6	1.5	2.8	5.3	2.0	3.3
General: Number	2,826	4,505	7,331	3,387	5,037	8,424	4,079	6,387	10,466	4,827	7,299	12,126	5,159	8,061	13,220
Percent	21.2	20.6	20.5	21.0	20.6	20.4	21.9	22.5	21.9	24.1	23.7	23.9	23.4	24.3	24.0
Household arts: Number	8	2,967	2,975	8	3,368	3,376	---	4,144	4,144	15	4,191	4,206	26	4,927	4,953
Percent	.06	13.6	8.3	.05	13.8	8.2		14.6	8.7	.08	13.6	8.3	.1	14.9	9.0
Industrial arts:[1] Number	1,744	1,150	2,894	2,385	881	3,266	3,056	1,080	4,136	3,306	1,327	4,633	3,753	777	4,530
Percent	13.1	5.2	8.1	14.9	3.6	7.9	16.4	3.8	8.6	16.5	4.3	9.1	17.1	2.3	8.2
Other: Number	135	40	175	9	132	141	134	59	193	30	140	170	27	264	291
Percent	1.0	.1	.5	.06	.5	.3	.7	.2	.4	.2	.5	.3	.1	.8	.5
Total	13,308	21,793	35,775	16,106	24,392	41,211	18,623	28,374	47,762	19,994	30,240	50,825	22,002	32,665	55,171

See footnotes at end of table.

TABLE 8.—*Curriculum registrations for the past 10 years in 207 high schools for Negroes, by sex*—Continued

Curriculum	1930-31			1931-32			1932-33			1933-34			1934-35		
	Male	Female	Total	Male	Female	Total	Male	Female	Total	Male	Female	Total	Male	Female	Total
	17	18	19	20	21	22	23	24	25	26	27	28	29	30	31
Academic or college preparatory:[1]															
Number	13,476	21,190	34,907	14,538	21,076	35,614	16,003	22,715	38,718	17,450	24,503	41,953	19,361	27,190	46,551
Percent	46.2	49.7	48.5	45.7	47.0	46.5	45.4	47.2	46.6	46.9	48.9	48.1	44.8	47.7	46.4
Agriculture:															
Number	428	82	510	577	108	685	555	101	656	589	112	701	788	184	972
Percent	1.5	.2	.7	1.8	.2	.8	1.6	.2	.8	1.6	.2	.8	1.8	.3	.9
Commercial:															
Number	984	2,002	2,986	1,212	2,198	3,410	1,333	2,426	3,759	1,400	2,497	3,897	1,606	2,874	4,480
Percent	3.3	4.7	4.1	3.8	4.9	4.4	3.8	5.0	4.5	3.8	4.9	4.5	3.7	5.0	4.5
Trades:															
Number	1,416	840	2,256	1,585	888	2,473	1,681	1,098	2,779	1,763	1,177	2,940	2,049	1,244	3,293
Percent	4.9	1.9	3.1	4.9	1.9	3.2	4.8	2.3	3.3	4.7	2.4	3.4	4.7	2.2	3.3
General:															
Number	8,293	11,294	19,587	8,785	12,682	21,467	9,986	13,503	23,489	10,629	13,811	24,440	12,284	15,738	28,022
Percent	28.5	26.5	27.2	27.6	28.3	28.1	28.4	28.1	28.2	28.5	27.6	27.9	28.4	27.6	27.9
Household arts:															
Number	60	6,244	6,304	21	6,714	6,735	17	7,175	7,192	58	6,742	6,800	102	8,336	8,438
Percent	.2	14.7	8.8	.06	14.9	8.8	.04	14.9	8.6	.2	13.5	7.8	.2	14.6	8.4
Industrial arts:[1]															
Number	4,430	745	5,175	5,041	845	5,908	5,583	920	6,533	5,306	1,092	6,398	6,950	1,313	8,263
Percent	15.2	1.7	7.2	15.9	1.9	7.7	15.9	1.9	7.8	14.2	2.2	7.3	16.1	2.3	8.2
Other:															
Number	55	223	278	44	331	375	50	130	180	48	132	180	56	147	203
Percent	.2	.5	.4	.1	.7	.5	.1	.3	.2	.1	.3	.2	.1	.3	.2
Total	29,142	42,620	72,003	31,803	44,842	76,667	35,208	48,068	83,306	37,243	50,066	87,309	43,196	57,026	100,222

[1] The following number of persons whose sex was not given were registered in the academic curriculum for the respective years: 1925–26, 674; 1926–27, 713; 1927–28, 765; 1928–29, 591; 1929–30, 504; 1930–31, 241. 22 such persons were registered in industrial arts curriculum in 1931–32, and 30 in 1932–33.

Vocational offerings in college.—The results of an inquiry concerning the number of colleges preparing teachers in specified vocational fields and the number preparing persons to engage in specified occupations are shown for public and private colleges, respectively, in tables 9 and 10. A larger number of both prepare teachers for the upper elementary grades than for any other field, the respective numbers being 21 and 14. Twenty public colleges prepare teachers of home economics; 19, of primary grades; and 17, of agriculture. Among the private colleges, 12 prepare high-school teachers; 11, primary teachers; 9, music teachers; and 8, teachers of home economics. The four courses offered by the largest number of public colleges for direct occupational preparation with the number offering each are: Agriculture, 18, home economics, 18, carpentry and woodworking, 15, and auto mechanics, 14. The four courses offered by the largest number of private colleges for direct occupational preparation are: Theology 10, pre-medical 8, home economics 7, and pre-dental 6.

TABLE 9.—*Number of public colleges offering Negro students specified vocational courses*

[Total number replying, 27]

Teacher education courses	Number of colleges	Direct vocational courses	Number of colleges
Academic subjects:		Agriculture	18
Grammar grade	21	Home economics	18
Primary	19	Carpentry and woodworking	15
High school	15	Auto mechanics	14
Kindergarten	2	Electricity	11
Home economics	20	Stenography and typewriting	11
Agriculture	17	Tailoring	11
Industrial arts	11	Masonry and plastering	10
Business administration	10	Printing	10
Stenography and typewriting	10	Business administration	9
Music	9	Music	9
Nursing	3	Painting	8
Library science	2	Plumbing	8
Trades:		Pre-medical	7
Carpentry and woodworking	11	Pre-dental	6
Auto mechanics	10	Pre-pharmacy	6
Electricity	9	Blacksmithing and iron work	5
Printing	9	Shoemaking and leather work	5
Masonry and plastering	8	Nursing	4
Tailoring	8	Pre-engineering	4
Plumbing	7	Pre-law	4
Shoemaking and leather work	6	Architecture	3
Laundering	4	General shop	3
Blacksmithing and iron work	3	Laundering	3
Interior decorating	2	Library science	3
Butler's course	1	Mechanical arts	3
Cosmetology	1	Upholstering	3
Machine shop industry	1	Beauty culture	2
Painting	1	Photography	2
Photographic	1	Building construction	1
Sheet metal	1	Ceramics	1
Upholstery	1	Commercial art	1
Welding	1	Commercial dietetics	1
		Interior decorating	1
		Journalism	1
		Ornamental concrete	1
		Physical education	1
		Poultry	1
		Power plant engineering	1
		Radio	1
		Welding	1
		Woodcrafts	1

TABLE 10.—*Number of private colleges offering Negro students specified vocational courses*

[Total number replying, 20]

Teacher-education courses	Number of colleges	Direct vocational courses	Number of colleges
Academic subjects:		Theology	10
Grammar grade	14	Pre-medical	8
High school	12	Home economics	7
Primary	11	Pre-dental	6
Kindergarten	4	Pre-pharmacy	6
Music	9	Business administration	5
Home economics	8	Music	5
Social administration	4	Pre-law	4
Business administration	3	Social administration	2
Stenography and typewriting	3	Stenography and typewriting	2
Nursing	1	Architecture	1
		Civil engineering	1
		Electrical engineering	1
		Mechanical engineering	1
		Nursing	1

Curriculum registrations in college.—The numbers of persons registered in certain vocational curriculums in public colleges, for each of the years from 1930 to 1935, are shown in table 11. In agriculture, architecture, and home economics the trends are downward in both percentages and numbers of students registered from 1930–31 to 1934–35. In nursing there is a slight increase in numbers, but a decrease in percentage of students registered. In business administration and trades there is an increase in both numbers and percentages of students registered in 1934–35 over 1930–31. While there is an increase in the number of students enrolled in all the vocational curriculums combined, the numbers being 28,925 and 33,123, for the years 1930–31 and 1934–35, respectively, there is a slight decrease in the percentage of the total enrollment registered in all vocational curriculums. The percentages for 1930–31 and 1934–35 are, respectively, 12.2 and 11.6.

Of the private colleges, only one reported courses in architecture and engineering, three in social administration and trades, and two in home economics. The numbers involved are too small to permit of reliable conclusions. However, it may be noted that there is a slight increase in numbers and percentages registered in architecture and engineering and in home economics, a considerable increase in social administration and in trades.

TABLE 11.—*Number of Negro students registered in vocational curriculums in certain colleges under public control, for each year from 1930–31 to 1934–35*

Curriculum	1930–31			1931–32			1932–33			1933–34			1934–35		
	Males	Females	Total	Males	Females	Total	Males	Females	Total	Males	Females	Total	Males	Females	Total
1	2	3	4	5	6	7	8	9	10	11	12	13	14	15	16
Agriculture:															
Total enrollment [1]	2,876	5,661	8,537	3,112	5,278	8,390	2,900	4,452	7,352	3,550	5,014	8,564	4,220	5,327	9,547
Curriculum registration	723	310	1,033	671		671	778		778	1,115		1,115	940		940
Architecture:															
Total enrollment	116	58	174	225	53	278	174	54	228	234	88	322	381	113	494
Curriculum registration	14		14	6		6	4		4	4		4	6		6
Business administration:															
Total enrollment	1,248	2,248	3,496	1,355	2,309	3,664	1,426	1,904	3,330	1,639	2,009	3,648	1,822	2,156	3,978
Curriculum registration	99	112	211	119	160	279	133	165	298	138	202	340	159	221	380
Home economics:															
Total enrollment	3,002	6,124	9,126	3,286	5,709	8,995	3,047	4,878	7,925	3,764	5,618	9,382	4,265	5,633	9,898
Curriculum registration	5	1,452	1,457		1,253	1,253		864	864	1	1,407	1,408		1,147	1,147
Nursing:															
Total enrollment	646	939	1,585	637	871	1,508	463	494	957	860	925	1,785	1,054	1,085	2,139
Curriculum registration		61	61		69	69		77	77		137	137		79	79
Trade:															
Total enrollment	2,167	3,840	6,007	2,299	3,807	6,106	2,153	2,976	5,129	2,619	3,559	6,118	3,036	4,031	7,067
Curriculum registration	745	9	754	773	14	787	847	10	857	865	27	892	1,287	26	1,313
Total vocational curriculum registration	1,586	1,944	3,530	1,569	1,496	3,065	1,762	1,116	2,878	2,123	1,773	3,896	2,392	1,473	3,865

[1] In colleges reporting: 16 schools are represented in agriculture; 18 in home economics; 6 in business administration; 1 in architecture; 3 in nursing; and 12 in trade.

Trends in vocational offerings in college.—The extent to which colleges are responsive to occupational trends is indicated by the courses added and dropped. Information on this matter was received from 15 public and 4 private institutions. Of 53 courses added by the 15 public institutions, 25 were added by 2, and of the 16 courses added by the 4 private institutions, 13 were added by one. In no case did more than one private college add a given course. The course added by the largest number of public colleges (5) was in the building trades; the course added by the next largest number of public colleges (4) was in auto mechanics.

Inquiry was made concerning the reasons courses were added. Among the private institutions, in every case except one, the courses were added upon the request of students. The reasons given for adding courses by the public institutions, with the number of institutions giving each, are as follows: By request of students, 18; occupational demands, 14; certification requirements, 7; to enrich curriculum offerings, 6; to provide elementary occupational training, 4; to encourage students to enter small industries, 4.

FEDERAL AID FOR VOCATIONAL EDUCATION

The first Morrill Act.—The first Morrill Act was for the purpose of establishing, in cooperation with the States, a system of scientific, technical, and practical higher education.[11] Passed in 1862, this Act made "no provision for racial division of students. The result was that the proceeds from the sale of the Federal grants of public land or scrip were devoted in most instances to the creation of endowments for the benefit of white institutions."[12] Thus, the aid given by the Federal Government to the development of vocational education on the collegiate level in the States, with the exception of four, was not shared by institutions for Negroes until the passage of the second Morrill Act in 1890. This Act specifically provides for equitable distribution of the Federal funds appropriated for the establishment of land-grant colleges, in the following provision:

> *Provided*, That no money shall be paid out under this act to any State or Territory for the support and maintenance of a college where a distinction of race or color is made in the admission of students, but the establishment and maintenance of such colleges separately for white and colored students shall be held to be a compliance with the provisions of this act if the funds received in such State or Territory are equitably divided as hereinafter set forth: *Provided*, That in any State in which there has been one college established in pursuance of the act of July second, eighteen hundred and sixty-two, and also in which an educational institution of like character has been established, or may be hereafter established, and is now aided by such State from its own revenue, for the education of colored students in agriculture and the mechanic arts, however named or styled, or whether or not it has received money heretofore under the act to which this act is an amend-

---

[11] Survey of Land-Grant Colleges and Universities. Washington, Government Printing Office, 1930. (United States Department of the Interior, Office of Education, Bulletin 1930, No. 9.)

[12] Ibid., p. 837.

ment, the legislature of such State may propose and report to the Secretary of the Interior a just and equitable division of the fund to be received under this act between one college for white students and one institution for colored students established as aforesaid, which shall be divided into two parts and paid accordingly, and thereupon such institution for colored students shall be entitled to the benefits of this act and subject to its provisions, as much as it would have been if it had been included under the act of eighteen hundred and sixty-two, and the fulfillment of the foregoing provisions shall be taken as a compliance with the provision in reference to separate colleges for white and colored students.

Each of the Southern States, very soon after the passage of this act, made provision for accepting its terms, either by establishing a land-grant college for Negroes, by converting an existing State institution into a land-grant college, or by transferring the funds which Negroes should receive to private institutions.

Even after provision was made for vocational education of Negroes on the collegiate level, by the arragements previously mentioned, its growth was slow. There were three major reasons for this. First, it required time for Negro students to leave the institutions with which they had become familiar and to change from the liberal arts program found in the private colleges. This resulted in few students in the land-grant colleges. In the second place, because of the limited public education facilities on the elementary and secondary school levels, these newly created "colleges" were compelled to devote most of their time and energies to education below college grade. Finally, because liberal arts training was more popular among Negroes than agricultural and mechanical training, because most of the administrators and teachers in the land-grant colleges were trained along liberal arts lines, and because there was no clear understanding of the purpose and meaning of the legislation establishing the land-grant colleges, emphasis was placed on classical training.

The Smith-Hughes Act.—On February 23, 1917 the Smith-Hughes Act was passed in order "to provide for the promotion of vocational education," including agriculture, trades and industries, and home economics. Supplementary acts have been passed providing for commercial training. The training provided by this act must be of less than college grade, for persons over 14 years of age, and specifically to aid persons toward competency in their occupational pursuits.

The general purpose of the act was stated by ex-President Hoover as follows:

> The essential purpose of the Smith-Hughes Act is to provide for the needs of our youths who do not enter our higher technical and professional educational institutions. Vocational training for the commoner wage-earning pursuits and skilled trades is equally as essential as is training for the professions. The humblest worker, equally with the youth who proposes to enter the professions, has a right to the sort of

training he needs for the occupation by which he proposes to earn his livelihood and support his family, and through which he will render his service to the community in getting the community's work done. We cannot in fairness continue to provide specialized education free to the few who propose to enter the professions, while denying education to the many for the commoner vocations.

There is in fact no better economy than the economy of adequate training for the pursuits of agriculture, commerce, industry, and the home. Our youth must enter into these pursuits, and it is on all counts in the public interest that they be well trained for them. To provide such training is clearly a public responsibility. Education in general, including vocational education for the youth, is democracy's most important business. Democracy in education means that in the field of education opportunity shall be extended equally to all—to give all a fair start. This is the educational ideal inspiring those who are administering the Federal Vocational Education Act; it is the ideal which inspired Congress in passing the Act; and it is traditionally the ideal of education in our democracy.

The grants under this act, for the country as a whole, in 1918 amounted to $1,855,586.72. In 1937 the grants amounted to $10,642,580.62. In 1937 the George-Deen Act was passed by Congress, "to provide for the further development of vocational education in the several States and Territories." The amount *authorized* to be appropriated annually under this act is $14,-750,000. Particular attention is called to the fact that, whereas the Smith-Hughes Act actually appropriated funds, the George-Deen Act merely authorizes, or makes possible, appropriations not exceeding the amount stipulated.

Distribution of funds among Negroes.—Under these acts the Federal Government does not propose to undertake the organization and direction of vocational education in the States, but does agree to make from year to year substantial financial contribution to its support. It undertakes to pay over to the States annually certain sums of money and to cooperate in fostering and promoting vocational education and the training of vocational teachers. The grants of Federal money are conditional, and the acceptance of these grants imposes upon the States specific obligations to expend the money paid over to them in accordance with the provisions of the acts.

This cooperation of the States with the Federal Government is based upon four fundamental ideas: (1) That vocational education being essential to the national welfare, it is a function of the National Government to stimulate the States to develop and maintain this service; (2) that Federal funds are required to adjust equitably among the States the burden of providing the service; (3) that since the Federal Government is vitally interested in the success of vocational education, it should, so to speak, secure a degree of participation in this work; and (4) that only by creating such a relationship between the central and the local governments can better and more uniform standards of educational efficiency be set up.[13]

---

[13] Statement of policies for the administration of vocational education. Washington, Government Printing Office, 1937 (Revised edition). (United States Department of the Interior, Office of Education. Vocational education bulletin 1937, No. 1.)

One of the purposes of the act, as shown in (2) in the above quotation, is to "adjust equitably among the States the burden of providing the service" (vocational education). However, no stipulation is made for securing equitability within the States, as far as classes for Negroes are concerned. A study of the distribution of the funds within the States indicates inequitability in provisions for courses in vocational subjects similar to that referred to in provision for high-school facilities.

Trends in use of Federal funds.—The proportion of funds allotted to schools for Negroes from the Federal funds for vocational education for specific purposes in 1934 compared with the ratio which they bear to the total population is shown in figure 2. In every State except one (Oklahoma) the percentage of expenditures is less than the ratio indicated. Also, it will be noted that the lines representing percentages of courses, enrollments, and teachers are, with few exceptions, consistently above the line representing expenditures.

There were encouraging increases in number of teachers and courses, and enrollments from 1928–29 to 1934–35 except during the most acute depression period (1931–33). Even then, there was an increase in enrollment of girls. Similarly, there were increases in expenditures, but the percentage increase was far less than in the other items, as shown by figure 3. In some cases the increases during this period in enrollment of Negroes in federally aided vocational courses exceeded corresponding increases for whites. Complete data for the Federally aided vocational work in high schools may be seen in tables I, II, III, and IV in appendix A.

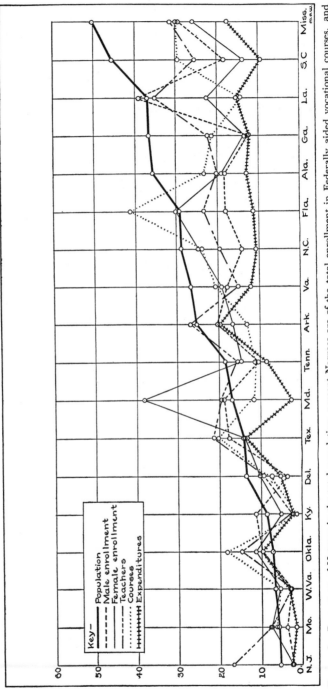

FIGURE 2.—Percentage of Negroes in the total population, percent Negroes are of the total enrollment in Federally aided vocational courses, and the percent of the total expenditures, courses, and teachers available to them in 18 States, 1934–35.

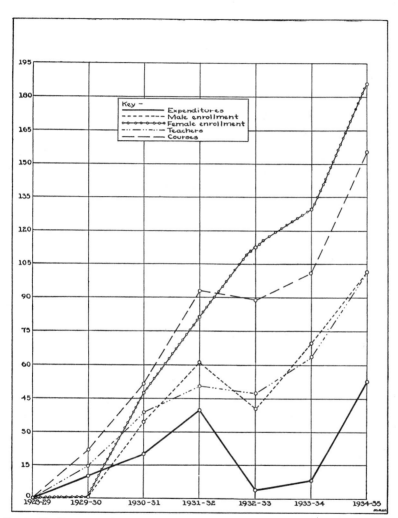

FIGURE 3.—Percentage increase or decrease in expenditures, in number of courses, in number of teachers, and in enrollments in Federally aided vocational work for Negroes, for each year from 1929–30 to 1934–35 compared with 1928–29, in 18 States.

CHAPTER IV

Vocational Education in Agriculture[1]

THE ADEQUACY of vocational education in agriculture for Negroes must be considered in light of the social and economic situation in rural areas and of the special relation of Negroes to it.

The application of machinery to the farm has caused revolutionizing changes. The successful farmer today must know how to handle machines and appliances, power for which is generated by wind, gas, water, steam, oil, and electricity. The application of chemistry to farm problems has made available an increased fund of scientific knowledge. Moreover, farming has become a highly competitive industry and calls for a high degree of managerial ability. Profitable distribution of farm products demands a knowledge of business and an appreciation of cooperative marketing. These conditions have brought about greater specialization of tasks, have increased the need for diversification of crops, and have made the farmer less self-sufficient. In addition to other social and economic conditions, these changes have been associated with decreasing farm population, increasing size of farms, and increased production per acre and per man.

The changes have affected Negroes particularly because they are still predominantly rural. According to the 1930 Census there were 11,891,143 Negroes in the United States. Of this number, 6,697,230, or 56.3 percent, lived in rural areas. The percentages living in rural areas in 1920 and 1910, respectively, were 66 and 72.7.

The following examples show the changes that have taken place among Negro farmers during the past decade:[2] (1) there has been a decrease of nearly half a million Negroes, or 6.2 percent, in the farm population, and of 42,858, or 4.6 percent, in the number operating farms. The number of Negro farmers per 1,000 Negro population fell from 88 in 1920 to 74 in 1930 as compared with a corresponding decrease for white farmers from 58 to 49 per 1,000 population. (2) The number of farms operated by Negroes in 17 Southern States decreased by 44,659, or 4.9 percent. (3)

---

[1] Data on federally aided vocational education in agriculture were taken from the State reports sent to the Vocational Education Division of the Office of Education.

[2] The Negro Farmer in the United States, Washington, Government Printing Office, 1930. (Fifteenth Census of the United States, 1930. Census of agriculture.)

There has been a decrease in the total acreage in farms operated by Negroes of 3,835,050 acres, or 9.3 percent in contrast to an increase of 34,943,840 acres, or 3.8 percent, in farms operated by whites. (4) The average size of farms operated by Negroes has decreased from 44.8 acres in 1920 to 42.6 acres in 1930. The average farm operated by white farmers increased in size during the same period from 165.7 to 176 acres. (5) The value of land and buildings of farms operated by Negroes decreased during the decade by $854,699,526, or 37.9 percent, while the decrease for whites during this same period amounted to $17,508,988,184, or 27.4 percent. (6) There was a decrease in Negro farm operators by each class of tenure as follows: Owners, 37,596, or 17.2 percent; managers, 1,103, or 54.4 percent; tenants, 4,159, or 0.6 percent. During this same period white owners decreased 8.8 percent, managers decreased 20.3 percent, and tenants increased 12.3 percent. The one item which increased during the decade under consideration was the value of implements and machinery owned by Negro farmers. The trends indicated here have important implications for educational programs for Negroes in rural areas.

NUMBER OF SCHOOLS AND CLASSES [3]

In general, vocational courses are offered in high school. Vocational instruction is offered in the upper grades of the elementary school in some communities, but it is not particularly effective. Such work cannot be carried on in most of the 1,726 rural schools offering 1 or more years of high-school work because of the limited facilities. Only about one-third of these schools participate in the Federal program for vocational education in agriculture.

The most common type of school providing vocational agricultural instruction for Negroes is the regular, all-day, county training school. The work is departmentalized, and that in agriculture is usually federally aided. A few other types of high schools, such as those connected with land-grant colleges and semiprivate schools, receive support from the State or county and share in the Federal vocational education program. In 1934–35 there were 542 all-day schools for Negroes receiving Federal aid for vocational education in agriculture in the 18 States where separate schools are maintained. Another type of school in which vocational courses in agriculture are offered is the day-unit school, a modification of the all-day school. "It differs from the departmental type only in the amount of agricultural instruction which is given, this being limited to certain selected units. This restriction is due to the fact that the teacher of agriculture must usually divide his time among several schools which are conveniently located, so that he can make the circuit at least once a week and preferably oftener."[4] In 1934 there were 264 such schools for Negroes.

---

[3] Unless otherwise indicated all data in this chapter refer to the 18 States maintaining separate schools for the Negro and white races.

[4] Sargent, H. O. Vocational Education in Agriculture for Negroes. Washington, Government Printing Office, 1926. (Federal Board for Vocational Education. Bulletin 1926, No. 111, Agricultural series, No. 28.)

Part-time schools are designed mainly for farm boys who have dropped out of all-day school and wish instruction in agriculture while farming. In 1934–35 there were 320 such schools in which Negro boys were enrolled. Still another type of school in which vocational education in agriculture is offered is the evening school. It is designed especially for adult farmers. There were 784 such schools for Negroes in 1934–35. In general, all of these different types of schools are operated in the same building and by the same teachers.

There is a consistent percentage increase in the number of all-day schools in which vocational agriculture is taught for each of the years from 1926–27 to 1934–35 over 1925–26. The number of classes in vocational agriculture for Negroes in the different types of schools increased 128.9 percent from 1928–29 to 1934–35. The percentage increase for each year from 1929–30 to 1934–35 over 1928–29 is shown below:

	1929–30	1930–31	1931–32	1932–33	1933–34	1934–35
Percent.....	27.4	42.3	91.8	65.3	83.5	128.9

The distribution of the classes among the different types of schools is shown in table 12.

TABLE 12.—*Number and percent of classes for Negroes in federally aided vocational agriculture, according to types of schools by years in 18 States*

Year and type of school	Number	Percent	Year and type of school	Number	Percent
1928–29:			1932–33:		
Evening	293	56.1	Evening	442	51.2
Part-time	101	19.3	Part-time	224	25.9
Day unit	128	24.5	Day unit	197	22.8
Total	522	---------	Total	863	---------
1929–30:			1933–34:		
Evening	400	60.1	Evening	559	58.3
Part-time	128	19.2	Part-time	225	23.4
Day unit	137	20.6	Day unit	174	18.1
Total	665	---------	Total	958	---------
1930–31:			1934–35:		
Evening	460	61.9	Evening	698	58.4
Part-time	126	16.9	Part-time	265	22.1
Day unit	157	21.1	Day unit	232	19.4
Total	743	---------	Total	1,195	---------
1931–32:					
Evening	583	58.2			
Part-time	229	22.8			
Day unit	189	18.8			
Total	1,001	---------			

CURRICULUM OFFERINGS AND REGISTRATIONS

All-day schools.—Courses in vocational agriculture in the federally aided all-day schools are offered in conjunction with the regular high-school courses. The high-school curriculums vary among the States as to content, but, in general, they consist of English, science, mathematics, foreign languages, social science, and the vocational subjects. It is prescribed by law establishing Federal aid for vocational education that "such schools or classes giving instruction to persons who have not entered upon employment shall require that at least half of the time of such instruction be given to practical work on a useful or productive basis, such instruction to extend over not less than 9 months per year and not less than 30 hours per week." This does not apply to agriculture. Because of the age and general nature of the purposes of the pupils in the all-day schools, the vocational subjects in agriculture deal with the fundamentals of farm life. In each of the States the vocational agriculture courses are based upon the farm enterprises of that specific region. The students are taught how to perform the operative and managerial jobs and solve the problems that are found on their own farms. Each student actually participates in the work of farming by operating and managing a farm program of his own.

TABLE 13.—*Number and percent of total Negro students registered in each kind of agricultural course, by type of school, 1934–35, in 18 States* [1]

Kind of course	Type of school					
	Evening		Part-time		Day-unit	
	Number	Percent	Number	Percent	Number	Percent
1	2	3	4	5	6	7
Animals, farm	273	1.5	42	1.1	56	1.4
Canning	165	.9				
Corn and corn products	919	5.1	319	8.3	1,043	26.4
Cotton	1,431	8.0	607	15.9	767	19.4
Crops and crop problems	788	4.3	362	8.4	277	7.0
Farm organization	535	2.9	63	1.6		
Farm reorganization	1,269	7.1				
Farm production	2,658	14.8	443	11.6	461	11.6
Farm records and management	2,267	12.7	426	11.1	17	.4
General farming	2,491	13.9	1,040	27.2	588	14.9
Hogs and hog production	163	.9	41	1.1		
Home implements	25	.1	25	.6	10	.2
Home orchard	16	.08				
Live-at-home	2,998	16.7	104	2.7	108	2.7
Markets and trucking	138	.7	210	5.5	121	3.0
Modern pioneers	9	.05	154	4.0		
New Deal problems	346	1.9				
Peanuts and alfalfa	40	.2	9	.2		
Poultry	969	5.4	67	1.7	213	5.4
Soil	642	3.5	55	1.3	24	.6
Total enrollment	17,859		3,805		3,944	

[1] Vocational Agriculture is no longer taught in day unit courses.

Other types of schools.—The types of courses in vocational agriculture offered in evening, part-time, and day-unit courses are shown in table 13. In the federally aided evening schools during 1934–35 there were registrations in 20 different courses. Students were registered in 16 different courses in the part-time school, and in 12 courses in the day-unit schools. The total number and percent of Negro students registered in the different federally aided vocational agricultural courses are also given in the table. The percents are computed from the total enrollment in that particular type of school. Instead of offering specific courses, some schools use the cross-sectional method of organizing their teaching materials rather than the unit courses. This means that a portion of all the farm enterprises may be taught throughout the entire course.

Of the 480 regular high schools for Negroes reporting to the Statistical Division of the Office of Education for 1934, enrollments in vocational courses in a given number of schools were as follows:

Course	Number of schools	Registration
General agriculture	142	4,211
Soils and crops	10	140
Animal husbandry	5	82
Farm mechanics	2	57

Of the 47,046 pupils enrolled in the 164 reorganized schools [5] reporting, 1,775, or 4 percent, were enrolled in general agriculture. The small registration in agriculture in the reorganized schools is probably due to the fact that most of them are in urban communities. While many of these schools are probably not participating in the federally aided vocational agricultural program, the data are significant from the guidance point of view in showing the possibilities for pre-vocational education and exploratory courses.

ENROLLMENTS IN TYPES OF SCHOOLS

Trends in enrollments in federally aided vocational agricultural courses in the different types of schools for Negroes from 1928–29 to 1934–35 may be traced in table 14. Although there is an increase in the number of males enrolled in all-day agricultural classes from 1928–29 to 1934–35, the percentage of the total enrollment decreased during the same period from 52.4 to 38.8. In evening agricultural classes there was an increase in the number of males enrolled of from 5,197 to 14,761, and an increase in the percentage of the total male enrollment from 29.9 to 40.2. Both number and percent of females enrolled in all-day schools decreased during this period, while there was a marked increase in the number and percent of females enrolled in evening schools; the former increased from 510 in 1928–29 to 3,098 in 1934–35; the latter from 57.4 to 93.5 percent.

---

[5] Organized on junior-senior high-school basis.

TABLE 14.—*Number and percent of Negro students enrolled in courses in vocational agriculture in the different types of federally aided schools, according to years, in 18 States*

Year and type of school	Males		Females	
	Number	Percent	Number	Percent
1	2	3	4	5
1928–29:				
All-day	9, 110	52. 4	200	22. 5
Evening	5, 197	29. 9	510	57. 4
Part-time	1, 371	7. 9	37	4. 2
Day unit	1, 689	9. 7	141	15. 9
Total	17, 367	----------	888	----------
1929–30:				
All-day	9, 512	52. 4	148	17. 1
Evening	5, 324	29. 3	572	66. 2
Part-time	1, 420	7. 8	6	.6
Day unit	1, 896	10. 4	137	15. 8
Total	18, 152	----------	863	----------
1930–31:				
All-day	10, 489	43. 5	264	13. 1
Evening	8, 969	37. 2	1, 585	78. 7
Part-time	2, 047	8. 4	8	.3
Day unit	2, 597	10. 7	156	7. 7
Total	24, 102	----------	2, 013	----------
1931–32:				
All-day	11, 542	40. 1	131	4. 9
Evening	11, 851	41. 2	2, 274	86. 2
Part-time	2, 840	9. 8	24	.9
Day unit	2, 526	8. 7	207	7. 8
Total	28, 759	----------	2, 636	----------
1932–33:				
All-day	10, 315	40. 2	142	8. 6
Evening	8, 502	33. 1	1, 321	80. 4
Part-time	3, 202	12. 4	74	4. 5
Day unit	3, 619	14. 1	105	6. 3
Total	25, 638	----------	1, 642	----------
1933–34:				
All-day	12, 688	40. 3	73	2. 8
Evening	12, 524	39. 8	2, 393	94. 0
Part-time	3, 233	10. 2	27	1. 0
Day unit	3, 013	9. 5	52	2. 0
Total	31, 458	----------	2, 545	----------
1934–35:				
All-day	14, 236	38. 8	94	2. 8
Evening	14, 761	40. 2	3, 098	93. 5
Part-time	3, 741	10. 2	34	1. 0
Day unit	3, 900	10. 6	87	2. 6
Total	36, 638	----------	3, 313	----------

Below will be found the percentage increase or decrease in enrollment in all types of schools offering courses in vocational agriculture for each year from 1929–30 to 1934–35 compared with 1928–29, for Negroes by sex.

	1929–30	1930–31	1931–32	1932–33	1933–34	1934–35
1	2	3	4	5	6	7
Male	4. 5	38. 8	65. 6	47. 6	81. 1	110. 9
Female	−2. 8	126. 7	196. 8	84. 9	186. 6	273. 1

A way to determine to what degree the federally aided vocational agriculture program is reaching the Negro farm boy is to compute the percentage that their agriculture enrollment in all-day, part-time, and day-unit schools is of the total number of rural Negro boys in the 14 to 20 year age groups attending school in the 18 States studied. According to data shown in table 14 there were in 1934–35, 21,877 boys enrolled in agriculture courses in all-day, part-time, and day-unit schools in these States. This enrollment constitutes 10.6 percent of the total males 14 to 20 years of age (205,731) attending school in these States. In 1924 the corresponding percentage was 4.[6] This shows considerable improvement in the proportion of Negroes reached.

THE COLLEGE PROGRAM

The land-grant colleges and a few private colleges have been the chief sources of instruction in agriculture for Negroes on the collegiate level. Practically all of the graduates of agriculture courses from these institutions enter the field of teaching or related work. The three major occupations followed by graduates of these colleges are: (1) Vocational teaching in high schools, (2) extension work, and (3) college teaching. This limited range is emphasized when the distributions of Negro and white graduates of 5 white and 10 Negro agricultural colleges according to occupations followed are compared, as in table 15. It is further shown by data given in table 16, which compares the percentage of Negro and white agricultural college graduates trained as teachers of vocational agriculture in the Southern States for 1935–36. For the regions as a whole the respective percentages are, for whites 41.2; for Negroes 91.6.

TABLE 15.—*Occupational distribution of the 1934 graduates majoring in agriculture of 5 white and 10 Negro agricultural colleges, Southern Region, 1935* [1]

Type of occupation	Graduates			
	Number		Percent	
	Negro	White	Negro	White
1	2	3	4	5
Agricultural extension service	2	16	1.7	9.5
Agricultural technicians		4		2.4
Commercial lines related to agriculture		12		7.0
Educational workers:				
College and experiment station workers	4	4	3.4	2.4
Graduate students and assistants		27		16.1
Vocational teachers	60	16	51.8	9.5
Other teachers	34	5	29.3	3.0
Forestry, lumbering, and park service		1		.6
Landscape gardening and floriculture	2		1.7	
Practical agriculture	2	29	1.7	17.3
Recovery and relief agencies	8	29	6.9	17.3
State Department of Agriculture		3		1.8
U. S. Department of Agriculture		5		3.0
Miscellaneous nonagricultural occupations	4	16	3.5	9.5
Unemployed or unaccounted for		1		.6
Total	116	168	100.0	100.0

[1] LeBeau, Oscar Ray. Factors Affecting the Need Among Negroes for Graduate Courses in Agriculture. Doctor's thesis. Ithaca, N. Y., Cornell University, 1936.

[6] Ibid., p. 13.

TABLE 16.—*Percent of agricultural college graduates trained as teachers of vocational agriculture by States, 1935–36* [7]

	Graduates	
State	White	Negro
Alabama	38. 7	73. 9
Arkansas	64. 3	100. 0
Florida	44. 8	94. 1
Georgia	53. 3	100. 0
Louisiana	51. 4	100. 0
Mississippi	38. 7	100. 0
North Carolina	34. 3	100. 0
Oklahoma	26. 9	90. 9
South Carolina	23. 1	100. 0
Tennessee	67. 7	100. .0
Texas:		
A. & M	29. 9	100. 0
Sam Houston	100. 0	
A. & I	100. 0	
Technological	60. 0	
Virginia	35. 7	
Ettrick		66. 7
Hampton		75. 0
Total	41. 2	91. 6

Curriculum offerings and registrations.—The courses offered in the agriculture curriculum by 16 public [8] institutions of higher learning and the registration in each for 1935–36 are given in table 17. New methods of accounting and new demands made on the farmer by changes in the credit system resulting from the operation of the Federal Farm Credit Administration, would suggest the need of rather large enrollments in subjects relating to accounting and credits. Of the 11,841 students enrolled in the 16 institutions reporting registrations in agricultural curriculums, 80 are registered in courses that are related to these subjects. A similar situation prevails with respect to the subjects dealing with problems of agricultural reorganization and cooperative marketing. Even if these topics are included in such subjects as marketing and farm organization the numbers enrolled are not in keeping with their growing importance.

Problem of preparing teachers.—Although practically all the Negro graduates of agriculture curricula from institutions of higher learning enter the field of teaching, as shown in table 18, reports from school officials indicate that the supply of trained Negro teachers in agriculture is inadequate. Enrollment in agricultural teacher-training courses increased 6.5 percent from 1928–29 to 1934–35. This slight increase is probably due to several things, some of which are lack of funds and lack of interest of school administrators. Chapter VII shows that the percentage of the total amount of Federal funds expended for the preparation of teachers received by institutions for Negroes ranged from 11.1 in 1928–29 to 16.1 in 1934–35.

---

[7] Data obtained from the Agricultural Education Service of the Vocational Education Division of the Office of Education.

[8] Hampton and Tuskegee are included here.

TABLE 17.—*Number of Negro students enrolled in specified courses in agriculture in 16 public institutions of higher learning,*[9] *1935–36*

Course	Enroll-ment	Course	Enroll-ment
Agricultural economics	105	Farm crops	59
Agricultural education	620	Farm finance	43
Agricultural engineering	123	Farm machinery and shop work	210
Agricultural chemistry	81	Farm management and organization	172
Agricultural journalism	81	Fruit growing	33
Agricultural judging	3	General agriculture	268
Agronomy	403	Genetics	40
Animal husbandry	454	Greenhouse management	5
Animal nutrition	31	Horticulture	512
Animal pathology	19	Household physics	9
Apprenticeship	13	Marketing	181
Bacteriology	145	Materials and mathematics in farm	
Cotton	18	shop	8
Crop diseases	15	Plant pathology	158
Dairying, cattle, and milk production	229	Poultry production	270
Economic geography	40	Power machinery	33
Economics, market, and farm produc-		Rural accounts	2
tion	29	Soils and fertility	182
Engines	7	Supervision	13
Entomology	25	Survey of agriculture	34
Extension methods	6	Veterinary science	140
Farm accounting	35	Vocational education and guidance	35

The number and percentage increase of Negro teachers of vocational agriculture in the different types of federally aided schools from 1928–29 to 1934–35 were as follows:

Type of school	Number	Percent
All-day	131	35
Evening	255	104
Part-time	207	265
Day-unit	130	194

Additional data[10] concerning these teachers are given in tables 18, 19, 20, and 21. Table 18 indicates that 52 percent of the Negro teachers trained in vocational agriculture in 1936 were placed as teachers of this subject, and that 25.7 percent were placed in other teaching positions. The percentage of Negro men trained as teachers of vocational agriculture who did not find work was 15.8. The apparent lack of enough teaching positions in vocational agriculture to absorb the Negroes trained in that field may be due among other things to—(1) Lack of schools of the kind in which vocational subjects can be taught; (2) lack of funds; and (3) lack of adequate demand for classes. In addition, Negro teachers frequently carry more than a normal load, which may keep other teachers out of a job. For example, data shown in tables 19, 20, and 21 indicate that a larger percentage of Negro teachers than white teachers conduct classes in all three

---

[9] Hampton and Tuskegee are included here. Total enrollment of all schools, 11,841.

[10] From the Agricultural Education Service of the Vocational Education Division of the Office of Education.

types of schools, namely, all-day, evening, and part-time; that the average number of classes per teacher is larger among Negro than among white teachers; and that a larger percentage of Negroes teach other subjects in addition to agriculture and also act as principals.

The above data indicate that more teachers would be needed if funds for vocational agriculture and number of schools in which it was offered were available, and the teaching load were improved.

TABLE 18.—*Placement of Negro men trained as teachers of vocational agriculture by States, 1935–36* [1]

State [2]	Total number of new teachers qualified	Placement of teachers trained, 1936—				Num- ber not placed	Outlook for 1937	
		As teachers of vocational agriculture		In other teach- ing posi- tions	In posi- tions other than teach- ing		Num- ber ex- pected to qualify	Estimated need
		In the State	Out of State					
Alabama	17	4	10	2	1	0	20	More than this year.
Arkansas	7	7	0	0	0	0	10	10 needed.
Florida	16	4	0	12	0	0	10	Probably sufficient.
Georgia	12	4	0	8	1	0	11	54 if funds available.
Louisiana	15	12	0	0	1	2	11	Sufficient unless new funds.
Mississippi	11	2	0	0	0	9	10	3 to 5.
North Carolina	9	3	1	1	3	1	20	Need strong.
Oklahoma	10	4	0	3	0	3	9	12 requests.
South Carolina	9	5	0	2	0	2	12	40 if funds available.
Tennessee	8	1	1	1	0	6	11	Depends on funds.
Texas	23	14	0	5	4	0	12	10 to 12 needed.
Virginia:								
Ettrick	8	4	1	3	0	0	11	Quite adequate.
Hampton	6	0	3	2	0	1	10	Probably sufficient.
Total	151	64	16	39	10	24	157	
Percent		42. 1	9. 9	25. 7	6. 6	15. 8	3. 3	

[1] Data obtained from the Agricultural Education Service of the Vocational Education Division of the Office of Education.
[2] Kentucky did not train Negro teachers of vocational agriculture.

TABLE 19.—*Kinds of classes conducted by teachers of vocational agriculture, fiscal year 1935–36*

Region	Total teachers of all- day classes	Teachers conducting—							
		All-day classes only		All-day and eve- ning classes		All-day and part- time classes		All-day, part- time, and eve- ning classes	
		Number	*Percent*	*Number*	*Percent*	*Number*	*Percent*	*Number*	*Percent*
1	2	3	4	5	6	7	8	9	10
Total	5, 474	2, 537	46. 34	1, 712	31. 27	562	10. 26	663	12. 11
North Atlantic	870	449	51. 60	87	9. 9	310	35. 63	24	2. 75
Southern:									
White	1, 834	372	20. 28	1, 082	58. 99	84	4. 58	296	16. 13
Negro	565	88	15. 57	183	32. 38	17	3. 01	277	49. 02
North Central	1, 605	1, 104	68. 78	301	18. 75	140	8. 72	60	3. 73
Pacific	600	524	87. 33	59	9. 83	11	1. 83	6	. 99

[1] Data obtained from the Agricultural Education Service of the Vocational Education Division of the Office of Education.

TABLE 20.—*Teaching load of teachers of vocational agriculture, 1935–36* [1]

Region	Number of teachers	Number of classes					Number of different classes taught by the average teacher during the year					
		All-day	Part-time	Evening	Day-unit	Nonvocational	All-day	Part-time	Evening	Day-unit	Nonvocational	Total
1	2	3	4	5	6	7	8	9	10	11	12	13
Grand total	5,469	12,910	1,306	3,587	530	4,013	2.36	0.24	0.68	0.10	0.73	4.11
Total, white only	4,904	11,769	1,008	2,938	327	3,407	2.40	.21	.60	.07	.70	3.98
North Atlantic	865	2,252	356	141	0	399	2.60	.41	.16	0	.46	3.63
Southern	1,834	4,428	419	2,320	327	362	2.41	.23	1.26	.18	.20	4.28
North Central	1,604	3,765	217	399	0	1,751	2.35	.14	.25	0	1.09	3.83
Pacific	601	1,324	16	78	0	895	2.23	.03	.13	0	1.49	3.88
Total, Negro only	565	1,141	298	649	203	606	2.02	.53	1.15	.36	1.07	5.13
Southern	550	1,107	298	632	203	587	2.01	.54	1.15	.37	1.07	5.14
Other regions	15	34	0	17	0	19	2.27	0	1.13	0	1.27	4.67

[1] Data obtained from the Agricultural Education Service of the Vocational Education Division of the Office of Education.

TABLE 21.—*Number of full-time and prorated teachers of all-day classes, fiscal year 1935–36* [1]

Region	Total teachers of all-day classes	Full-time teachers		Prorated teachers [1]															
				Total		Teaching 1 other subject		Teaching 2 other subjects		Teaching 3 other subjects		Serving as principal		Serving as principal and teaching one other subject		Serving as principal and teaching 2 other subjects		Having other prorating arrangements	
		Number	Percent	Number	Percent	Number	Percent	Number	Percent	Number	Percent	Number	Percent	Number	Percent	Number	Percent	Number	Percent
1	2	3	4	5	6	7	8	9	10	11	12	13	14	15	16	17	18	19	20
Total	5,469	3,249	59.4	2,220	40.6	475	21.4	570	25.7	254	11.4	417	18.8	68	3.1	102	4.6	334	15.1
North Atlantic	865	604	69.9	261	30.1	113	43.3	58	22.2	25	9.6	16	6.1	11	4.2	5	1.9	33	12.6
Southern:																			
White	1,834	1,490	81.2	344	18.8	116	33.7	40	11.6	20	5.8	124	36.0	5	1.5	14	4.1	25	7.3
Negro	564	214	37.9	350	62.1	19	5.4	24	6.9	17	4.9	140	40.0	20	5.7	30	8.6	100	28.6
North Central	1,605	729	45.4	876	54.6	142	16.2	335	38.2	135	15.4	123	14.0	23	2.6	40	4.6	78	8.9
Pacific	601	212	35.3	389	64.7	85	21.9	113	29.0	57	14.7	14	3.6	9	2.3	13	3.3	98	25.2

[1] Data obtained from the Agricultural Education Service of the Vocational Education Division of the Office of Education.
[2] A prorated teacher is one who is performing duties other than vocational teaching.

FEDERAL AID FOR VOCATIONAL AGRICULTURAL EDUCATION

Federal expenditures for agriculture in all types of schools from 1928–29 to 1934–35 in 18 States are given in table 22. The proportion of funds allotted to schools for Negroes ranged from 8 to 12 percent for the different years. The range in all-day schools, where most of the money is spent, was from 7.6 to 11.6 percent. The percentage increases and decreases in schools for Negroes in Federal expenditures, enrollment, and in the number of courses and teachers in vocational agriculture from 1929–30 to 1934–35 compared with 1928–29 are shown in figure 4.

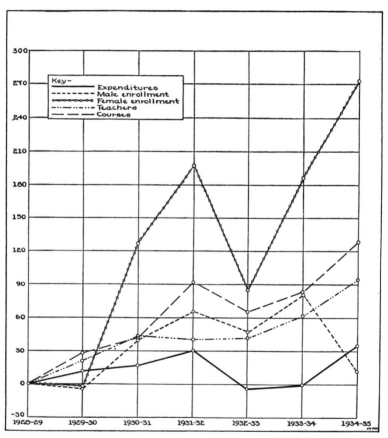

FIGURE 4.—Percentage increase or decrease in enrollments, number of courses, and teachers, and expenditures in Federally aided agricultural classes each year from 1929–30 to 1934–35 compared with 1928–29, in 18 States

TABLE 22.—*Amount and percent of Federal funds expended for vocational agriculture in the different types of schools, according to race and years, in 18 States*

Type of school	1928–29		1929–30		1930–31		1931–32	
	Amount	Per-cent	Amount	Per-cent	Amount	Per-cent	Amount	Per-cent
1	2	3	4	5	6	7	8	9
All-day:								
White	$1,242,530.81	89.0	$1,351,416.04	88.8	$1,957,632.33	91.7	$2,473,609.54	92.4
Negro	153,081.05	10.9	171,194.09	11.2	177,107.54	8.3	204,044.52	7.6
Evening:								
White	35,913.84	78.8	37,648.86	78.2	44,510.36	79.0	25,492.86	72.8
Negro	9,660.46	21.2	10,523.77	21.8	11,802.44	21.0	9,522.00	27.2
Part-time:								
White	2,712.49	68.2	1,624.24	39.5	75.00	4.9	0.00	
Negro	1,267.47	31.8	1,062.50	60.5	1,449.41	95.1	2,050.00	100.0
Day-unit:								
White	10,911.00	80.6	5,923.45	62.2	9,147.51	70.5	5,418.60	77.3
Negro	2,634.09	19.4	3,594.07	37.8	3,835.77	29.5	1,595.00	22.7
Total:								
White	1,292,068.14	88.5	1,396,612.59	88.2	2,011,365.20	91.2	2,504,521.00	92.0
Negro	166,643.07	11.5	186,374.43	11.8	194,195.16	8.8	217,211.52	8.0
Grand total	1,458,711.21	------	1,582,987.02	------	2,205,560.36	------	2,721,732.52	------

Type of school	1932–33		1933–34		1934–35	
	10	11	12	13	14	15
All-day:						
White	$1,251,696.44	89.2	$1,190,904.95	88.4	$1,647,954.07	88.7
Negro	151,519.64	10.8	156,331.47	11.6	209,861.97	11.3
Evening:						
White	17,533.56	71.4	16,176.55	67.9	28,650.02	69.6
Negro	7,029.50	28.6	7,654.66	32.1	12,540.04	30.4
Part-time:						
White	0	------	750.00	70.1	5,554.41	83.0
Negro	63.00	100.0	262.50	29.9	1,135.27	17.0
Day-unit:						
White	2,653.58	67.7	4,402.20	75.7	4,613.00	73.7
Negro	1,264.00	32.3	1,412.50	24.3	1,650.00	26.3
Total:						
White	1,271,883.58	88.8	1,212,233.70	87.9	1,686,771.50	88.2
Negro	159,876.14	11.2	165,661.13	12.1	225,187.28	11.8
Grand total	1,431,759.72	------	1,377,894.83	------	1,911,958.78	------

CONCLUSIONS

In formulating a program in vocational education for Negroes in rural areas problems growing out of their educational, social, and economic status should be considered. This chapter is devoted chiefly to educational problems. Obviously the extent to which the federally aided program is helpful is conditioned by the number of youth and adults reached by it. This depends on the number of children who have enough general education to profit by the program and the number and accessibility of schools in which a federally aided program is offered.

A condition which affects any education program for Negroes is the literacy situation. In 1930, 20.5 percent of the rural nonfarm and 23.2 percent of the rural farm population were illiterate, in contrast to 9.2 percent of the urban Negro population. The educational level of Negroes must be raised if they are to benefit fully from the instruction offered to meet new occupational demands.

In 1930 in the United States there were 803,373 Negroes in rural areas 15 to 19 years of age—12 percent of the total rural Negro population. The number is considerably larger than the urban Negro population of the same age group. Most of these young people are in the South, the number in the North and West being only 26,355. Taking the country as a whole, there are 2,004,082 Negroes 12 to 19 years of age, 1,316,204 of whom were rural, potential candidates for training in useful occupations. In order adequately to meet this need for training, two provisions are necessary: First, additional high schools for Negroes which participate in the Federal vocational education program; second, additional part-time and evening schools to bring educational facilities to the large number of Negro children gainfully employed as well as to those out of school and not employed. Data on this subject as they pertain to rural areas are given in a recent Office of Education study.[11] This study also shows that 5.48 percent of 48,707 pupils in rural areas were enrolled in high-school grades. Ninety-four percent of these children, therefore, do not have access to the vocational education opportunities in high school. Mollette found in 1932 that 80,000 Negro boys and girls in Georgia (90 percent of the school population) settled down on farms after completing the sixth grade without any formal training in agriculture.[12]

Pending the reduction of the number of Negro children in rural areas who are overage and who drop out of school early, it may be desirable to introduce vocational guidance and preparation in the upper grades of the elementary school. This might benefit overage pupils and provide vocational preparation for pupils who otherwise would not receive it.

---

[11] Availability of Education to Negroes in Rural Communities. Op. cit., pp. 8 and 63.

[12] Mollette, L. S. Agriculture in Negro Schools. Southern Workman, 61: 338–40, August 1932.

CHAPTER V

Vocational Education in Home Economics

NUMBER OF SCHOOLS AND CLASSES

All-day schools.—Home economics education has been developed in high schools under various circumstances, and in many cases under conditions which precluded Federal aid, consequently, relatively few schools offer federally aided vocational education in home economics. However, more schools than those listed below as receiving Federal aid are offering work in the field. According to the present investigation in 1934–35, there were 225 all-day schools for Negroes in the 18 States studied offering vocational education in home economics with Federal aid. This is a 543 percent increase over the 35 such schools in 1928–29. The number and percent of increase of all-day schools for each designated year over 1928–29 follow:

	1929–30	1930–31	1931–32	1932–33	1933–34	1934–35
Number of schools	55	70	107	128	183	225
Percent	57	100	205	265	423	543

Evening and part-time schools.—Data were not collected on the number of evening and part-time schools for federally aided vocational education in home economics. However, the availability of such instruction through these schools may be indicated by the number of classes offered. Table 23 shows that in 1934–35, 508, or 97 percent, of the classes offered in these two types of schools for Negroes were offered in evening schools. This is an increase of 316 percent over the number of such classes offered in 1928–29. Data presented in the table show also that the total number of classes offered in the evening schools increased consistently each year from 1928–29 to 1934–35. The trend noted above is significant because the training which adults receive in these classes can be put to immediate use in their homes. Moreover, it has an important influence on other members of the family, especially on those girls who do not take such training in the all-day school.

TABLE 23.—*Number and percent of classes for Negroes in federally aided home economics, according to types of schools and years, in 18 States*

Year and type of school	Number	Percent	Year and type of school	Number	Percent
1	2	3	1	2	3
1928–29: Evening	122	100. 0	1932–33:		
1929–30: Evening	160	100. 0	Evening	399	99. 5
1930–31:			Part-time	2	. 5
Evening	263	99. 6	1933–34: Evening	387	100. 0
Part-time	1	. 4	1934–35:		
1931–32:			Evening	508	96. 9
Evening	405	99. 5	Part-time	16	3. 0
Part-time	2	. 5			

CURRICULUM OFFERINGS AND REGISTRATIONS

Curriculum offerings in high schools.—The home-economics courses offered in 1934–35 in federally aided evening and part-time schools are listed in table 24. While certain duplication exists, some slight indication of the availability of these courses may be gained from the enrollments. In view of the facts concerning infant mortality and general health status of Negroes one would expect to find larger enrollments in courses on child care and nursing and hygiene. Similarly, enrollments are not large in parent education, although some instruction may be given in this subject in certain other courses.

TABLE 24.—*Number and percent of total Negro students registered in each kind of home economics course by type of school (1934–35), in 18 States*

Course	Type of school			
	Evening		Part-time	
	Number	Percent	Number	Percent
1	2	3	4	5
Child care	1, 076	10. 2	124	27. 8
Clothing	4, 131	39. 4	267	59. 8
Domestic service training	401	3. 8		
Family and community relation	901	8. 6		
Foods	2, 538	24. 2	20	4. 4
Gardening	158	1. 5		
Home economics, general			52	11. 6
Home furnishing	159	1. 5		
Home management	1, 734	16. 5		
Millinery and art	200	1. 9	23	5. 1
Nursing and hygiene	683	6. 5		
Parent education	44	. 4		
Total	10, 475		446	

Curriculum and course registrations in high schools.—In the 207 high schools selected for special study, about 14 percent of the girls were enrolled in household arts (home economics) curriculums in 1934–35. The percentages of the total enrollment of girls registered in these courses during the 10-year period from 1925–26 to 1934–35 [1] ranged from 13.6 to 14.9. In a study made by Jessen [2] of 609,893 pupils in nine States it was found that in 1922, 14.9 percent of the total enrollment was registered in home economics. In 1928 the corresponding percentage was 20.3. The registrations of Negroes in the home economics courses in federally aided departments are given in table 24, and in table 25 for schools reporting to the Office of Education for the regular quadrennial statistical study made by the office.

TABLE 25.—*Number of schools reporting and number and percent of Negro pupils registered in specified home economics courses in regular and reorganized high schools, 1934* [1]

Course	Regular high schools			Reorganized high schools		
	Number of schools reporting	Course registration		Number of schools reporting	Course registration	
		Number	Percent		Number	Percent
1	2	3	4	5	6	7
Child care	3	81	0.1			
Clothing	25	1,828	3.3	21	3,926	8.3
Cooking	27	1,718	3.1	12	1,626	3.5
Foods—nutrition, dietetics, cafeteria and tea room management	29	1,961	3.5	17	2,333	5.0
Family relationships	4	53	.09			
General home economics [2]	201	12,215	21.8	73	8,823	18.8
Home nursing	6	237	.4			
Laundry				6	404	.9
Sewing	36	2,234	4.0	13	1,667	3.5
Total number of schools reporting vocational subjects in high schools and total enrollment in such schools	335	56,096		131	47,046	
Total number of schools reporting and total enrollment in such schools	480	66,504		164	50,933	

[1] Schools for Negroes making the quadrennial report to the Statistical Division of the Office of Education, most of them being in the Southern States.
[2] Many of the specialized courses listed here are included in this course.

Course registrations in colleges.—Data were gathered on course registrations from 18 colleges under public control and 2 privately supported. These data are given in table 26. While it is difficult to ascertain the exact nature of many of the courses from the titles given, there appears to be greater emphasis than in the high schools, insofar as that can be judged by registrations, on certain modern problems in homemaking.

[1] See ch. III, table 8.
[2] Jessen, Carl A. Secondary Education. *In* Biennial survey of education, 1926–1928. Washington, Government Printing Office, 1930. United States Department of the Interior, Office of Education, Bulletin 1930, No. 16, ch. VI.

TABLE 26.—*College enrollment in specified home economics courses, in 18 public colleges and 2 private colleges for Negroes* [3]

Course	Enrollment	Course	Enrollment
Applied arts	68	House care and renovation	35
Beauty culture [4]	51	House planning and furnishing	157
Cafeteria management [4]	10	Household accounts	20
Child care and home nursing	400	Household chemistry	66
Clothing and textiles	622	Household economics	231
Clothing selection and construction	283	Household physics	38
Costume designing and art appreciation	482	Housing and equipment	58
Dairying	19	Hygiene	52
Education and directed teaching	297	Institutional management [4]	8
Experimental cookery	14	Interior decorating	58
Fancy cookery	4	Millinery designing	16
Food selection, preparation, serving, and preserving	1,018	Nutrition and dietetics	267
Family relations	6	Nursing and first-aid	67
Gardening and floriculture	19	Poultry and gardening	76
Home crafts	39	Practice cottage	57
Home economics materials and methods of observation	12	Problems of consumer buying	15
Home management and problems	235	Quantity food preparation and catering [4]	19
Horticulture	13	Tailoring [4]	11
		The family	21
		Weaving	3

ENROLLMENTS IN TYPES OF SCHOOLS

Data on enrollment in all types of schools are shown in table 27. Most of the federally aided courses in vocational education in home economics are given in all-day and evening schools. Few boys are enrolled in home economics courses in these schools, although large numbers of Negro men are engaged in occupations related to homemaking.

The percentage of the total female enrollment in all types of schools enrolled in the all-day schools increased from 31.4 in 1928-29 to 46.1 in 1934–35, while the corresponding percentage in evening schools decreased during the same period from 68.5 to 51.9. Female enrollments in all-day and evening schools increased markedly from 1928–29 to 1934–35, the percentage increases for the respective years are: All-day, 333; evening, 124. The percentage increases and decreases in female enrollments in home economics courses in all types of federally aided schools each year from 1929–30 to 1934–35 compared with 1928–29 are shown below:

Percentage increase of enrollment compared with 1928–29

	1929–30	1930–31	1931–32	1932–33	1933–34	1934–35
Percent	—1.0	45.2	80.9	120.8	128.9	195.3

Percentages are shown graphically in figure 5.

These data show significant increases during the 7-year period. They do not, however, show the relation to the actual need for such courses. In 1934–35, 10,416 Negro girls were enrolled in federally aided home

---

[3] Total enrollment for 18 public colleges, 12,833; total enrollment for 2 private colleges, 2,107.

[4] Not strictly home economics courses, ordinarily taught as trade courses.

economics courses in all-day schools. This number is 4 percent of all Negro girls 15 to 19 years of age in the 18 States studied.

TABLE 27.—*Number and percent of Negro students enrolled in home-economics courses in the different types of federally aided schools, according to years, in 18 States*

Year and type of school	Males		Females	
	Number	Percent	Number	Percent
1	2	3	4	5
1928–29:				
All-day			2,406	31.4
Evening	72		5,243	68.5
Part-time				
Total	72		7,649	
1929–30:				
All-day			2,784	36.8
Evening			4,786	63.2
Part-time				
Total			7,570	
1930–31:				
All-day			3,257	29.3
Evening			7,797	70.2
Part-time			51	.5
Total			11,105	
1931–32:				
All-day			4,531	32.7
Evening	30		9,264	66.9
Part-time			44	.3
Total	30		13,839	
1932–33:				
All-day	6	54.5	5,905	34.9
Evening	5	45.4	10,806	64.0
Part-time			180	1.1
Total	11		16,891	
1933–34:				
All-day	91	59.9	9,105	51.9
Evening	61	40.1	8,407	48.0
Part-time				
Total	152		17,512	
1934–35:				
All-day	114	79.7	10,416	46.1
Evening	29	20.3	11,728	51.9
Part-time			446	1.9
Total	143		22,590	

That relatively few women and girls enrolled in part-time schools, as shown in table 27, is probably due to the fact that the federally aided part-time vocational work in home economics is listed with and is administered by the departments of trades and industries in the different States. In general, it is supervised by the regular home-economics supervisors having charge of the all-day programs. Thus, there is maintained a close relation between the general trades and home-economics work. The enrollment in the part-time schools offering trades and industries in home-economics courses is shown in chapter VI, table 34. Few Negro females are enrolled in these part-time courses.

NUMBER OF TEACHERS

The number of Negro teachers of home economics in all types of federally aided schools increased 177 percent from 1928–29 to 1934–35. The number in the all-day schools increased during the same period from 50 to 231, or 362 percent; in evening schools from 136 to 276, or 103 percent. In many cases the all-day teachers of home-economics courses in federally aided departments also teach courses in the evening schools. Sometimes additional compensation is granted for this extra service or a reduction is made in number of classes in the all-day program.

From 1928–29 to 1932–33 there were fewer pupils per teacher in the white all-day schools; from 1933–34 to 1934–35, fewer pupils per teacher among Negro schools. In the evening schools for each of the years studied there were fewer pupils per teacher among schools for Negroes. (See table 28.)

TABLE 28.—*Pupil-teacher ratio in federally aided home-economics courses in all-day and evening schools, according to race and years*

Type of school	1928–29			1929–30			1930–31			1931–32		
	Female enrollment	Number of teachers	Ratio	Female enrollment	Number of teachers	Ratio	Female enrollment	Number of teachers	Ratio	Female enrollment	Number of teachers	Ratio
1	2	3	4	5	6	7	8	9	10	11	12	13
All-Day:												
White	8, 061	263	30. 6	15, 217	419	36. 0	22, 168	580	38. 2	29, 426	891	33. 0
Negro	2, 406	50	48. 1	2, 784	63	44. 1	3, 257	80	40. 7	4, 531	120	37. 8
Evening:												
White	26, 399	465	56. 8	31, 124	531	58. 6	37, 553	596	63. 0	50, 160	705	71. 1
Negro	5, 243	136	38. 6	4, 786	149	32. 1	7, 797	188	41. 5	9, 264	254	36. 5

Type of school	1932–33			1933–34			1934–35		
	Female enrollment	Number of teachers	Ratio	Female enrollment	Number of teachers	Ratio	Female enrollment	Number of teachers	Ratio
	14	15	16	17	18	19	20	21	22
All-Day:									
White	42, 240	998	42. 3	56, 913	1, 139	50. 0	82, 602	1, 637	50. 4
Negro	5, 905	138	42. 8	9, 105	192	47. 4	10, 416	231	45. 1
Evening:									
White	48, 822	490	99. 6	41, 566	543	76. 5	43, 490	655	66. 4
Negro	10, 806	233	46. 4	8, 407	218	38. 6	11, 728	276	42. 5

FEDERAL AID FOR VOCATIONAL EDUCATION IN HOME ECONOMICS

The amount of Federal funds expended to reimburse States for instruction in home economics is given in table 29. The percentage of the total Federal funds for home economics allotted to schools for Negroes each year ranges from 8.2 to 10.2. The percentage increase of expenditures for home-economics instruction in classes for Negroes for each of the succeeding 6 years over 1928–29 is greater than the corresponding percentage increases

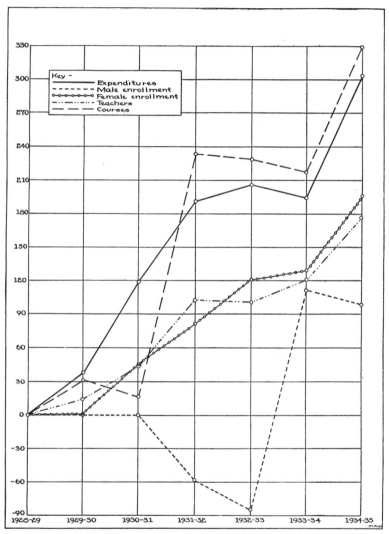

Key –
——————— Expenditures
– – – – – – Male enrollment
o-o-o-o-o-o Female enrollment
—··—··—··· Teachers
— — — Courses

FIGURE 5.—Percentage increase or decrease in enrollments, number of courses and teachers, and expenditures in Federally aided home economics classes each year from 1929–30 to 1934–35 compared with 1928–29, in 18 States.

in the number of courses, enrollment, and number of teachers, as shown in figure 5.

TABLE 29.—*Amount and percent of Federal funds expended for home economics in the different types of schools, according to race and years, in 18 States*

Type of school	1928–29		1929–30		1930–31		1931–32	
	Amount	Per-cent	Amount	Per-cent	Amount	Per-cent	Amount	Per-cent
1	2	3	4	5	6	7	8	9
All day:								
White	$68,709.28	89.1	$148,824.40	92.7	$243,073.90	93.7	$338,101.16	92.9
Negro	8,432.39	10.9	11,733.01	7.3	16,408.89	6.3	25,654.06	7.1
Evening:								
White	52,968.21	90.7	63,093.30	89.5	68,471.03	83.9	90,260.24	46.5
Negro	5,409.02	9.3	7,423.71	10.5	13,125.45	16.1	13,910.90	53.5
Part-time:								
White	472.22	------	1,145.10	------	1,017.83	91.1	3,515.76	82.4
Negro	------	------	------	------	100.00	8.9	749.16	17.6
Total:								
White	122,149.71	89.8	213,062.80	91.8	312,562.76	91.3	431,877.16	91.5
Negro	13,841.41	10.2	19,156.72	8.2	29,634.34	8.7	40,314.12	8.5
Grand total	135,991.12	------	232,219.52	------	342,197.10	------	472,191.28	------

Type of school	1932–33		1933–34		1934–35	
	Amount	Per-cent	Amount	Per-cent	Amount	Per-cent
	10	11	12	13	14	15
All day:						
White	$337,105.46	91.9	$301,472.40	90.6	$483,588.25	91.6
Negro	29,721.32	8.1	31,364.60	9.4	44,417.92	8.4
Evening:						
White	68,365.23	84.6	52,897.38	84.9	58,148.81	84.9
Negro	12,431.52	15.4	9,431.58	15.1	10,292.35	15.0
Part-time:						
White	6,418.55	97.3	5,581.52	------	9,503.42	89.3
Negro	180.00	2.7	------	------	1,132.87	10.7
Total:						
White	411,889.24	90.7	359,951.30	89.8	551,240.48	90.8
Negro	42,332.84	9.3	40,796.18	10.2	55,843.14	9.2
Grand total	454,222.08	------	400,747.48	------	607,083.62	------

CONCLUSIONS

Because of the economic status of Negroes and the effects of the disorganization of their family life during slavery, homemaking education for them is of special importance. Its need is shown by the prevalence [5] of poor health, inadequate housing, early marriage, mothers gainfully employed, and infant mortality among Negroes. Of the 2,405 high schools for Negroes in the 18 States studied, 225, or 9.3 percent, participated in the federally aided home economics program in 1934–35.

[5] U. S. Census, 1930. Op. cit.

Fundamentals in the Education of Negroes. Washington, Government Printing Office, 1935. (United States Department of the Interior, Office of Education, Bulletin 1935, No. 6.)

The major objective of homemaking education is improving home and family life. However, instruction in this field is related to certain occupations in which men and women are engaged. Many persons may use home economics instruction, especially that of high-school grade, as an introduction to vocational education in related fields. Domestic and personal service occupations is a case in point. The need of preparation for this occupation is shown by the number of Negroes employed. There were, in 1930, 1,152,-560 Negro women 10 years old and over gainfully employed in domestic and personal service. This is 62.6 percent of all gainfully employed Negro women. Negro men engaged in this group of occupations number 423,645 or 11.6 percent of the total Negro men gainfully employed in all occupations In 1930, Negroes constituted 28.6 percent of all domestic and personal service workers. This is an increase over the two preceding decades when the corresponding percentages were 22 and 21.6, respectively, for 1920 and 1910. Since so large a percentage of Negro workers are employed in these occupations, and since the demands in personal service occupations are increasing in number and complexity,[6] the school, through home economics instruction or some other agency, should definitely address itself to the task of preparing persons for effective adjustments in these occupations.

Improvement in the preparation of domestic and personal service workers will aid in improving the conditions of employment in this field, where there is a lack of standardization in wages, hours, duties, equipment, and materials, and in the relation between employee and employer. It has been said that household occupations are "the least standardized, the least modernized, the most feudal of all the work in the modern world." [7]

---

[6] Recent Social Trends in the United States (report of the President's researc committee on social trends). New York, McGraw-Hill Book Co., inc., 1933.

[7] Johnson, B. Eleanor. Household Employment in Chicago. Washington, Government Printing Office, 1933. (Women's Bureau, Bulletin No. 106.)

Household Employment Problems (a handbook for round-table discussions among household employers). Washington, United States Department of the Interior, September 1937. (Office of Education, Vocational Division, Misc. 1971.)

=======[*CHAPTER VI*]=======

Vocational Education in Trades and Industries

NUMBER OF SCHOOLS AND CLASSES

THERE WERE 61 all-day schools offering federally aided vocational courses in the 18 States studied in trades and industries for Negroes in 1934–35. This is an increase of 21, or 52.5 percent, over 1928–29. The number and percent increase or decrease of these schools for each year from 1929–30 to 1934–35 compared with 1928–29 are shown below:

	1928–29	1929–30	1930–31	1931–32	1932–33	1933–34	1934–35
Number	40	35	33	53	31	52	61
Percent		−12. 5	−17. 5	32. 5	−22. 5	30. 0	52. 5

Number of classes.—The number of federally aided classes in trades and industries in the different types of schools for Negroes is given in table 30. There was a total of 3,554 classes in trades and industries in 1934–35; 331 are for Negroes, most of them in evening schools. There was an increase in 1934–35 in the total number of classes for Negroes of 108 percent over 1928–29.

CURRICULUM OFFERINGS AND REGISTRATIONS

Curriculum offerings in high schools.—Federally aided courses in schools for Negroes in trades and industries are listed in table 31. White pupils are registered in 24 different courses in the all-day schools; Negroes in 12. In the federally aided evening schools, white students are registered in 36 different courses; Negroes in 14. White students are registered in 33 different part-time and trade extension courses; Negroes in 8.

Trades and industries courses offered by the schools reporting regularly to the Office of Education are shown in table 32.

58

TABLE 30.—*Number and percent of classes in federally aided trades and industries, according to types of schools and years, in 18 States*

Type of school by year	Number	Percent	Type of school by year	Number	Percent
1	2	3	1	2	3
1928–29:			1931–32—Continued.		
Evening	127	79. 9	Part-time general continuation	10	4. 1
Part-time trade extension and trade preparation	10	6. 3			
Part-time general continuation	22	13. 8	Total	242	-------
			1932–33:		
Total	159	-------	Evening	194	76. 4
			Part-time trade extension and trade preparation	45	17. 7
1929–30:					
Evening	134	87. 6	Part-time general continuation	15	5. 9
Part-time trade extension and trade preparation	12	7. 8			
Part-time general continuation	7	4. 5	Total	254	-------
			1933–34:		
Total	153	-------	Evening	203	75. 2
			Part-time trade extension and trade preparation	50	18. 5
1930–31:					
Evening	189	89. 6	Part-time general continuation	17	6. 3
Part-time trade extension and trade preparation	13	6. 2			
Part-time general continuation	9	4. 2	Total	270	-------
			1934–35:		
Total	211	-------	Evening	262	79. 1
			Part-time trade extension and trade preparation	58	17. 5
1931–32:					
Evening	215	88. 8	Part-time general continuation	11	3. 3
Part-time trade extension and trade preparation	17	7. 0	Total	331	-------

TABLE 31.—*Number of students registered in federally aided high-school vocational courses in trades and industries, according to race, 1934–35, in 18 States*

Type of course	Evening schools		Part-time trade extension courses		All-day schools	
	White	Colored	White	Colored	White	Colored
1	2	3	4	5	6	7
Aeronautics	305	-------	46	-------	517	-------
Architecture	978	8	168	-------	948	207
Auto mechanics	588	315	1, 018	36	2, 041	294
Blacksmithing	12	-------	-------	12	-------	-------
Blue-print reading	1, 305	11	118	-------	-------	-------
Board making	54	-------	-------	-------	-------	-------
Boatbuilding	-------	-------	-------	-------	30	-------
Boiler work	104	-------	40	-------	-------	-------
Bricklaying	83	36	1	46	171	150
Building trades	-------	-------	-------	-------	785	85
Cabinetmaking	166	53	41	-------	355	-------
Carpentry and woodwork	291	157	358	334	1, 233	495
Commercial art	709	38	181	-------	-------	-------
Electricity	1, 055	-------	469	-------	1, 219	100
Fire fighting	1, 385	-------	507	-------	-------	-------
Foremanship	74	-------	25	-------	-------	-------
Flour making	-------	-------	75	-------	-------	-------
General mechanics	1, 430	-------	101	-------	-------	-------
Greenhouse work	-------	-------	-------	-------	49	-------
Harnessmaking	-------	-------	37	-------	-------	-------
Illumination	-------	-------	23	-------	-------	-------
Internal-combustion engines	213	-------	-------	-------	-------	-------
Ironwork	-------	-------	39	-------	-------	-------
Janitor service	325	79	162	80	-------	-------
Machine shop	614	-------	816	-------	1, 147	118
Marble carving	-------	-------	70	-------	-------	-------

TABLE 31.—*Number of students registered in federally aided high-school vocational courses in trades and industries, according to race, 1934–35, in 18 States*—Continued

Type of course	Evening schools		Part-time trade extension courses		All-day schools	
	White	Colored	White	Colored	White	Colored
1	2	3	4	5	6	7
Masonry					132	325
Metal trades	285	9	144		632	
Mining	1,988	334	434			
Natural gas	20					
Painting	55		52		267	43
Petroleum industry			2,774			
Plumbing	109	11	96		57	
Pottery making			39		14	
Power-plant operation	52					
Practical engineering	16					
Printing	177		284		1,226	28
Pulp and paper making	477					
Radio mechanics	636	26	300	7	264	
Refrigeration and air conditioning	189		98		40	
Shipbuilding			659			
Shoemaking and repairing		124	407	21	98	126
Sign painting					89	
Steel making	100					
Surveying	11					
Tailoring	91	153			14	82
Textiles	2,639		662		102	
Tree surgery	14					
Upholstering	12					
Welding	530		195	1	152	

TABLE 32.—*Number of schools reporting and number and percent of Negro pupils registered in specified trades and industries courses in regular and reorganized high schools, 1934*

Course	Regular high schools			Reorganized high schools		
	Number of schools reporting	Course registration		Number of schools reporting	Course registration	
1	2	3	4	5	6	7
		Number	*Percent*		*Number*	*Percent*
Auto mechanics	7	796	1.4	5	305	0.6
Basketry				1	54	.1
Brick masonry	8	457	.8	2	152	.3
Carpentry and cabinetmaking	5	580	1.0	15	1,870	3.9
Chair caning				1	47	.09
Electric shop				3	369	.8
Industrial arts	88	5,478	9.8	58	8,664	18.4
Mechanical drawing	39	2,182	3.9	34	3,791	8.1
Machine shop				1	127	.3
Printing	5	614	1.1	6	577	1.2
Sheet metal and metal art	2	57	.1	5	504	1.1
Shop work	10	676	1.2	1	33	.07
Woodwork	5	296	.5			
Art [1]				3	845	1.8
Freehand drawing [1]	30	1,227	2.2	36	11,677	24.8
Total number of schools reporting vocational subjects in high schools and total enrollment in such schools	335	56,096		131	47,046	
Total number of schools reporting and total enrollment in such schools	480	66,504		164	50,933	

[1] Probably should be considered as related or prevocational courses.

Curriculum offerings in colleges.—Data received from 10 public colleges on courses offered in trades and industries curriculums are shown in table 33. Relatively few students are registered in most of the courses. Only eight persons are registered in the courses on labor problems. Judging the content by the titles of courses, there is an apparent lack of interest on problems relating to employee-employer relationships, and principles governing modern economic development.

TABLE 33.—*Number of Negro college students registered in specified vocational courses in industrial arts, architecture, and building construction curriculums*

Industrial Arts Curriculum [1]

Title of course	Enrollment	Title of course	Enrollment
Auto mechanics	107	Masonry	47
Business administration	14	Painting	7
Building construction	13	Physical measurements	37
Cabinetmaking, woodworking, and		Plumbing and heating	3
upholstering	210	Printing	6
Care of equipment	8	Radio	19
Ceramics	18	Safety hygiene	1
Commercial art	203	Sheet metal and welding	39
Drafting	6	Shop practice and management	148
Electricity	79	Surveying	50
Engineering	74	Tailoring	37
Forging	5	Typewriting	1
Labor problems	8	Vocational guidance	19
Manual training	9	Vocational and industrial education	250

Architecture and Building Construction Curriculum [2]

Title of course	Enrollment	Title of course	Enrollment
Applied mechanics	5	Field management	3
Appreciation of architecture	5	History of architecture	1
Architectural designing	21	Landscape planning	5
Builders' accounting	4	Ornamental drawing	6
Building construction practice	11	Painting	6
Building estimating	3	Principles of construction	1
Building materials	4	Secretarial studies	2
Building specifications	3	Shades and shadows	6
Building surveying	3	Strength of materials	6
Business principles	3	Structural designing	3
Carpentry	7	Water colors	6
Elements of architecture	6		

Curriculum and course registrations in high schools.—The percentage of the total enrollment of pupils registered in vocational and prevocational courses in the 207 high schools selected for special study was low. The range of the percentages for boys and girls combined from 1925–26 to

---

[1] 10 public schools represented, with a total enrollment of 7,818.

[2] 2 public schools represented, with a total enrollment of 2,663.

1934–35 was from 2.2 to 3.4. The range for the boys separately was from 4.3 in 1926–27 to 5.3 in 1929–30. In the study [3] previously referred to for both 1922 and 1928, 12.6 percent of the pupils were registered in manual training (probably the same as the courses discussed here).

The number of pupils registered in federally aided courses in trades and industries is shown in table 31. The schools reporting regularly to the Office of Education report course registrations as indicated in table 32. This table shows that 335 of the 480 regular schools reported registrations in trades and industries courses. The total enrollment in these schools was 56,096. As in the selected high schools, the percentage of the total enrollment registered in any one of the different courses is small. A considerably larger percentage of the pupils in reorganized schools is registered in industrial arts and mechanical and freehand drawing than in the regular schools.

According to data gathered from three sources, namely, the special study of 207 high schools included in this survey, the federally aided schools, and the schools reporting to the Statistical Division of the Office of Education, the following conclusions seem justified: The range of federally aided courses in trades and industries offered in secondary schools for Negroes is limited in comparison with the total number of courses offered; and in many of those offered relatively few Negroes are enrolled.

ENROLLMENTS IN TYPES OF SCHOOLS

In 1928–29 Negro males enrolled in federally aided vocational courses in trades and industries numbered 4,232. The percentage increases or decreases for each year from 1929–30 to 1934–35 compared with 1928–29 are given below. Similar data concerning other items are shown in figure 8.

The percentage increase or decrease of Negro enrollment compared with 1928–29

	1929–30	1930–31	1932–32	1932–33	1933–34	1934–35
Males	−12. 6	22. 7	49. 4	16. 5	29. 2	70. 1
Females	3. 4	20. 1	42. 4	103. 5	107. 7	138. 8

The enrollments in all-day schools, listed in table 34, constitute only a small fraction of the Negro high-school pupils in the States under consideration. The enrollments in the other types of schools show only a small fraction of those engaged in occupations in trades and industries. Moreover, the rapid migration of Negroes to urban centers indicates that schools in these communities should provide facilities preparing for urban occupations. The percentage of Negro girls and women enrolled in part-time general continuation classes in all types of schools is small in view of the relation between home economics and trades and industries instruction mentioned in chapter V.

---

[3] Secondary Education. Op. cit., ch. 5.

TABLE 34.—*Number and percent of Negro students enrolled in trades and industries courses in the different types of federally aided schools, according to year, in 18 States*

Year and type of school	Males		Females	
	Number	Percent	Number	Percent
1928–29:				
All-day	1,922	45.4	441	19.3
Evening	1,687	39.9	1,352	59.1
Part-time trade, extension and preparatory	348	8.2	243	10.6
Part-time general continuation	275	6.3	250	10.9
Total	4,232	---------	2,286	---------
1929–30:				
All-day	2,235	60.4	449	18.9
Evening	1,367	36.9	1,233	52.1
Part-time trade, extension and preparatory	19	.5	598	25.3
Part-time general continuation	79	2.1	84	3.5
Total	3,700	---------	2,364	---------
1930–31:				
All-day	2,663	51.3	520	17.5
Evening	2,274	43.8	2,051	68.9
Part-time trade, extension and preparatory	127	2.4	315	10.6
Part-time general continuation	127	2.4	87	2.9
Total	5,191	---------	2,973	---------
1931–32:				
All-day	3,423	54.1	611	18.8
Evening	2,696	42.6	2,156	66.2
Part-time trade, extension and preparatory	113	1.8	411	12.6
Part-time general continuation	92	1.4	77	2.4
Total	6,324	---------	3,255	---------
1932–33:				
All-day	2,495	50.5	835	17.9
Evening	2,153	43.6	2,510	53.9
Part-time trade extension and preparatory	197	4.0	1,031	22.2
Part-time general continuation	86	1.7	276	5.9
Total	4,931	---------	4,652	---------
1933–34:				
All-day	3,334	60.9	391	8.2
Evening	1,871	34.2	2,582	54.4
Part-time trade, extension and preparatory	93	1.7	1,372	28.8
Part-time general continuation	171	3.1	404	8.5
Total	5,469	---------	4,749	---------
1934–35:				
All-day	3,991	55.4	519	9.5
Evening	2,650	36.8	3,402	62.3
Part-time trade, extension and preparatory	441	6.1	1,322	24.2
Part-time general continuation	115	1.5	216	3.9
Total	7,197	---------	5,459	---------

NUMBER OF TEACHERS

The number of Negro teachers of trades and industries in all types of federally aided schools increased 84 percent from 1928–29 to 1934–35. The increases for the different types of schools during the same period were: All-day 57, or 66 percent; evening 124, or 95 percent; part-time trade extension 44, or 314 percent. In the part-time general continuation there was a decrease of 13, or 77 percent.

FEDERAL AID FOR VOCATIONAL EDUCATION IN TRADES AND INDUSTRIES

The amount of Federal funds allocated to reimburse States for instruction in vocational courses in trades and industries is given in table 35. The percentage of expenditures in all-day schools for Negroes is less since the depression than before, though the enrollment is larger. (See figure 6.)

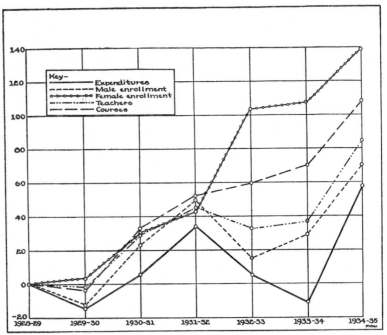

FIGURE 6.—Percentage increase or decrease in enrollments, number of courses and teachers, and expenditures in Federally aided trades and industries classes each year from 1929–30 to 1934–35 compared with 1928–29, in 18 States.

TABLE 35.—*Amount and percent of Federal funds expended for vocational work in trades and industries in the different types of schools, according to race and years, in 18 States*

Type of school	1928–29		1929–30		1930–31		1931–32	
	Amount	Per-cent	Amount	Per-cent	Amount	Per-cent	Amount	Per-cent
1	2	3	4	5	6	7	8	9
All-day:								
White	$149,038.45	88.8	$158,480.83	90.6	$159,930.46	89.2	$174,197.20	86.6
Negro	18,775.81	11.2	16,465.17	9.4	19,372.79	10.8	27,002.39	13.4
Evening:								
White	134,648.05	94.5	144,526.51	95.8	133,210.09	94.8	121,871.56	93.4
Negro	7,778.98	5.5	6,361.50	4.2	7,361.96	5.2	8,635.94	6.6
Part-time trade exten-sion:								
White	80,225.85	98.2	85,106.73	98.5	64,659.03	95.2	76,552.30	96.4
Negro	1,485.88	1.8	1,300.25	1.5	3,262.46	4.8	2,812.14	3.6
Part-time general con-tinuation:								
White	145,657.27	98.9	158,340.62	99.3	163,735.37	99.2	170,408.83	99.3
Negro	1,618.85	1.1	1,157.50	.7	1,330.22	.8	1,229.64	.7
Total:								
White	509,569.62	94.5	546,454.69	95.6	521,534.95	94.3	543,029.89	93.3
Negro	29,659.52	5.5	25,284.42	4.4	31,327.43	5.7	39,680.11	6.7
Grand total	539,229.14	------	571,739.11	------	552,862.38	------	582,710.00	------

	1932–33		1933–34		1934–35	
	10	11	12	13	14	15
All-day:						
White	$198,437.80	91.3	$186,977.26	93.6	$364,637.72	93.3
Negro	18,996.95	8.7	12,734.47	6.4	26,152.12	6.7
Evening:						
White	91,725.39	91.4	86,371.08	90.5	123,031.03	90.2
Negro	8,579.48	8.6	9,049.64	9.5	13,392.39	9.8
Part-time trade extension:						
White	77,100.73	96.5	72,829.96	95.3	144,299.22	96.8
Negro	2,822.95	3.5	3,568.60	4.7	4,809.59	3.2
Part-time general continuation:						
White	148,223.67	99.6	122,272.92	99.2	177,962.84	98.7
Negro	665.86	.4	952.80	.8	2,400.76	1.3
Total:						
White	515,487.59	94.3	468,451.22	94.7	809,930.81	94.5
Negro	31,065.24	5.7	26,305.51	5.3	46,754.86	5.5
Grand total	546,552.83	------	494,756.73	------	856,685.67	------

CONCLUSIONS

Three important facts are brought out in this chapter. First, relatively few courses are offered; second, few enroll in many of them; and, third, a small amount of Federal funds is allotted to schools for Negroes for instruction in trades and industries. While it is recognized that a certain amount of the Federal vocational education appropriations for trade and industrial courses must be used in part-time classes for employed workers, the possibility of increasing the opportunities for Negroes to receive such training within the limitations should be explored. The three facts mentioned have important implications in light of the following occupational conditions among Negroes.

According to census data and other studies,[4] a large percentage of Negroes engaged in trades and industrial occupations are unskilled, and according to a study made by the Vocational Education Division of the Office of Education, there is less and less place in the economic world for the ignorant, unskilled worker. While much of the required skill demanded today must be secured on the job, the school should assist in increasing the number of skilled Negroes by providing a greater number and variety of courses and by adapting its instruction to changing conditions. In this way it may furnish a larger number the background and point of view for meeting the demands of modern economic life.

Moreover, it can assist in providing that flexibility and in developing those personality traits which the President's Committee on Recent Social Trends suggested were increasingly in demand in our modern industrial society. Two ways of developing an individual's ability to make adjustments to meet the new demands and rapid shifts taking place in occupational life are: To give him a thorough elementary education and to teach him one occupation as thoroughly as possible and the rudiments of another. It is believed that, in general, persons who are prepared to do more than one thing well frequently make occupational adjustments more easily and quickly than those who know how to do only one thing.

Because of the complexity of the elements underlying occupational shifts, schools should be cautious in adding and dropping courses without careful study of the census data, the occupational situation in the community, and the interests and needs of the students concerned. In this connection, it is well for Negro students, teachers, and counselors to know that Negroes are engaged in many highly skilled occupations, generally with success.[5] Informing Negroes of such successful persons, of instances where the use of individual initiative and creativeness assisted in opening opportunities or bringing promotion, and of means by which Negroes have succeeded in overcoming racial barriers in industry will not only give them a broader occupational outlook but will also make necessary an enriched educational program for guidance in the selection of and preparation for effective occupational adjustment.

---

[4] Recent Social Trends in the United States. Op. cit.

Frazier, Edward K. Earnings of Negroes in the Iron and Steel Industry. Monthly Labor Review, 44: 3, 564–79, March 1937.

[5] Recent social trends in the United States. Op. cit.

CHAPTER VII

Teachers and Teaching

PREPARATION, EXPERIENCE, AND SALARIES

Academic preparation.—The median number of years of college and graduate education possessed by teachers of the different vocational subjects in the schools included in this investigation is as follows: Agriculture, 4.68; commerce, 1.11 (years of graduate work); home economics, 4.39; trades and industries 4.09; and theory and practice, 1.77 (years of graduate work). The median for all teachers combined (1,001 cases) is 4.48. In table 36 are shown the number and percentage of vocational teachers studied holding given degrees, classified according to the type of institution in which teaching is done.

TABLE 36.—*Number and percent of vocational teachers of Negroes studied who hold designated degrees, 1935–36, according to where they teach*

Type of institution	Degree held									
	A. B.	B. S.	M. A.	M. S.	Ph. D.	Other bachelor degrees	Other master degrees	Other degrees	Professional degrees	Total
1	2	3	4	5	6	7	8	9	10	11
Land-grant and other colleges:										
Number	3	24	24	20	3	4	10			88
Percent	3.4	27.3	27.3	22.7	3.4	4.5	11.3			100.0
Private high schools:										
Number	2	11				1	1	1		16
Percent	12.5	68.7				6.2	6.2	6.2		100.0
Trade schools:										
Number	5	11		2				2		20
Percent	25.0	55.0		10.0				10.0		100.0
Proprietary schools:[1]										
Number	1	4	2			2	1			10
Percent	10.0	40.0	20.0			20.0	10.0			100.0
Public high schools:										
Number	82	246	64	8	3	22	8	2	5	440
Percent	18.6	55.9	14.5	1.8	0.7	5.0	1.8	0.5	1.1	100.0
Total:										
Number	93	296	90	30	6	29	20	5	5	574
Percent	16.2	51.6	15.7	5.2	1.0	5.0	3.5	0.9	0.9	100.0

[1] Those schools operated by a proprietor, such as commercial colleges, schools of beauty culture, etc.

Occupational training.—Specialized training of teachers in the subjects taught was studied. According to the data, home-economics teachers have more training in their specialized field than those in the other fields studied, the median number of semester hours' credit being 38.89 as compared with 27.43 for teachers of commerce, 30 for teachers of agriculture, 30.14 for teachers of theory and applied science, and 30.81 for teachers of trades and industries. The median for all teachers combined is 41.71. Only 67 teachers in land-grant colleges replied to this particular question. According to the data obtained, they have less special vocational and more academic training than the high-school teachers studied.

Experience and tenure of teachers.—Information concerning teaching experience and tenure of vocational teachers of Negroes studied is shown in tables 37 and 38. Data concerning occupational experience were also collected (details not shown here). The median number of years of teaching experience is 6.86. Teachers with little training have been teaching longer than those with a greater amount, according to these data. Although only 49 teachers reported who had 4 years or less of high-school training, they had been teaching 15.29 years. The median years of experience decreases as the level of education increases. The percentage of vocational teachers of Negroes having a given amount of occupational experience other than teaching is as follows: 1 year, 12.8; 2 years, 8.3; 3 years, 21.2; 4 years, 14.5; 16 years or more, 20.8. The percentage of teachers remaining in their present position 6 to 10 years is higher than that in any other of the periods used in this classification.

TABLE 37.—*Median number of years of teaching experience of vocational teachers of Negroes according to educational level attained, 1935–36*

Educational level attained	Median years of experience	Number of cases
4 years of high school or less	15.29	49
6 weeks to 2 years of college	13.75	134
3 to 4 years of college	11.23	259
1 year or more of graduate work	4.58	216
Total	6.86	658

Age and salary of vocational teachers.—Information concerning the age of vocational teachers was received from 834 teachers. The median age for the entire group was 37.3 years. The range in the medians in the various subject fields was as follows: Agriculture, 36.3; commerce, 35.7; home economics, 35.2; trades and industries, 39.2; and theory and practice, 35.

In table 39 is shown the number of vocational teachers receiving annual salaries within a given range and the median annual salary received by teachers of given subjects. The median for all teachers combined is $1,871.74. The median annual salary ($1,851.85) of teachers of theory and applied sciences is higher than the medians in the other subjects studied; the lowest median ($1,060) is that received by the teachers of agriculture.

TABLE 38.—*Number and percent of vocational teachers of Negroes studied, employed a given number of years in the schools in which they are now working, 1935–36*

Type of institution	In present position—								Total
	Less than 1 year	1 year	2 years	3 to 5 years	6 to 10 years	11 to 15 years	16 to 30 years	31 or more years	
1	2	3	4	5	6	7	8	9	10
Land-grant and other colleges:									
Number		21	9	17	39	12	4	2	104
Percent		20.2	8.6	16.3	37.5	11.5	3.8	1.9	100.0
Private high schools:									
Number		4	1	1	7	7	3	1	24
Percent		16.6	4.2	4.2	29.2	29.2	12.5	4.2	100.0
Trade schools:									
Number		5		6	11	12	9		43
Percent		11.6		13.9	25.6	27.9	20.9		100.0
Proprietary schools:									
Number	1	9	4	11	10	7	3		45
Percent	2.2	20.0	8.8	24.4	22.2	15.5	6.6		100.0
Public high schools:									
Number	15	76	56	138	244	136	135	9	809
Percent	1.8	9.4	6.9	17.1	30.2	16.8	16.7	1.1	100.0
Total:									
Number	16	115	70	173	311	174	154	12	1,025
Percent	1.6	11.2	6.8	16.8	30.3	16.9	15.0	1.2	100.0

TABLE 39.—*Distribution of vocational teachers of Negroes, according to annual salary and subjects taught, 1935–36*

Subjects taught	Salary range									Total	Median
	$200–$400	$401–$600	$601–$800	$801–$1,000	$1,001–$1,200	$1,201–$1,400	$1,401–$1,600	$1,601–$1,800	Over $1,800		
1	2	3	4	5	6	7	8	9	10	11	12
Agriculture		1	1	6	5	2	3	1		19	$1,060.00
Commerce		6		3	8	2	7	12	46	84	1,817.39
Home economics	5	27	34	35	27	12	14	6	63	223	1,077.77
Trades and industries	3	15	17	30	14	22	13	24	159	297	1,813.21
Theory and applied science	1	1	3	2	3	2	11	3	54	80	1,851.85
Total	9	50	55	76	57	40	48	46	322	703	1,871.74

FEDERALLY AIDED TEACHER-TRAINING PROGRAM

Nearly all Negro vocational teachers are trained in federally aided classes, which are usually conducted by the land-grant colleges. Data concerning enrollments and expenditures in these classes are shown in tables 40 and 41. The number and percentage of Negro students enrolled in teacher-training classes in the vocational subject fields for each year from 1928 to 1934 are given in table 40. A majority of the male students is enrolled in agricultural teacher-training classes, and a majority of female students in home economics teacher-training classes. A very small percentage is enrolled in trades and industries classes. From 1928–29 to 1934–35 the increases in male enrollees in teacher-training classes were as follows: Agriculture, 6.6; trades and industries, 80. For female enrollees in home economics the corresponding increase was 58.7.

In 1928–29 there were 39 full-time teachers and 1 half-time teacher of subjects in the federally aided teacher-training programs for Negroes, in 1934–35 the number was 41. The corresponding numbers in each of the subject-matter fields are given below:

Subject	1928–29	1934–35
Agriculture	15½	21
Trades and industries	4	2
Home economics	20	18

TABLE 40.—*Number and percent of Negro students enrolled in federally aided vocational teacher-training work in the different subject-matter fields, by years in 18 States*

Year and type of school	Male		Female	
	Number	Percent	Number	Percent
1	2	3	4	5
1928–29:				
Agricultural	304	91.0	1	0.3
Trade and industry	30	9.0	34	11.4
Home economics			264	88.3
Total	334		299	
1929–30:				
Agricultural	346	85.6		
Trade and industry	58	14.4	51	10.8
Home economics			422	89.2
Total	404		473	
1930–31:				
Agricultural	281	76.4		
Trade and industry	15	4.1	44	13.7
Home economics	72	19.6	278	86.3
Total	368		322	
1931–32:				
Agricultural	310	78.5		
Trade and industry	85	21.5	46	9.9
Home economics			418	90.1
Total	395		464	
1932–33:				
Agricultural	327	82.9		
Trade and industry	67	17.0	73	17.2
Home economics			351	82.8
Total	394		424	
1933–34:				
Agricultural	121	38.3		
Trade and industry	[1] 195	61.7	96	13.5
Home economics			614	86.5
Total	316		710	
1934–35:				
Agricultural	324	85.7		
Trade and industry	54	14.3		
Home economics			419	100.0
Total	378		419	

[1] Apparent inconsistency here is due to the fact that 1 State reported duplicate registrations in courses instead of total enrollment in subject field.

TABLE 41.—*Amount and percent of Federal funds expended for the different subject-matter fields in federally aided teacher-training work, according to race and years, in States having separate schools*

Type of school	1928–29		1929–30		1930–31		1931–32	
	Amount	Per-cent	Amount	Per-cent	Amount	Per-cent	Amount	Per-cent
1	2	3	4	5	6	7	8	9
Agricultural:								
White	$99,025.19	88.9	$91,657.80	86.8	$88,890.56	85.8	$143,296.50	89.4
Negro	12,415.46	11.1	13,891.72	13.2	14,720.72	14.2	16,997.03	10.6
Trade and industrial:								
White	63,596.37	96.9	59,438.08	94.7	53,605.13	99.1	62,111.62	96.6
Negro	2,032.73	3.1	3,342.50	5.3	471.92	.9	2,201.20	3.4
Home economics:								
White	74,845.60	89.8	76,471.23	90.0	73,866.58	89.4	82,669.30	89.5
Negro	8,514.06	10.2	8,465.89	10.0	8,788.14	10.6	9,658.14	10.5
Total:								
White	237,467.16	91.2	227,567.11	89.9	216,362.27	90.1	288,077.42	90.9
Negro	22,962.25	8.8	25,700.11	10.1	23,980.78	9.9	28,856.37	9.1
Grand total	260,429.41	------	253,267.22	------	240,343.05	------	316,933.79	------

Type of school	1932–33		1933–34		1934–35	
	10	11	12	13	14	15
Agricultural:						
White	$87,570.37	86.8	$85,076.29	89.6	$87,618.63	83.9
Negro	13,310.95	13.2	9,878.99	10.4	16,760.15	16.1
Trade and industrial:						
White	60,081.11	96.6	57,440.94	96.3	61,826.12	97.1
Negro	2,124.22	3.4	2,207.04	3.7	1,840.25	2.9
Home economics:						
White	72,389.71	85.1	66,581.24	89.9	81,953.01	90.6
Negro	12,676.31	14.9	7,504.96	10.1	8,548.61	9.4
Total:						
White	220,041.19	88.7	209,098.47	91.4	231,397.76	89.5
Negro	28,111.48	11.3	19,590.99	8.6	27,149.01	10.5
Grand total	248,152.67	------	228,689.46	------	258,546.77	------

The total amount expended for federally aided teacher-training in the various States studied for 1928–29 and 1934–35 for the Negro and white races is given in table 42. It will be noted that in many cases the percentage increases of expenditures for Negroes in 1934–35 over 1928–29 are large, though the amounts are relatively small.

TABLE 42.—*Amount and percent of Federal expenditure for vocational teacher training during 1928–29 and 1934–35, and increase or decrease of 1934–35 compared with 1928–29, by State and by race, in 18 States*

State	1928-29 White Amount	1928-29 White Percent	1928-29 Negro Amount	1928-29 Negro Percent	1934-35 White Amount	1934-35 White Percent	1934-35 Negro Amount	1934-35 Negro Percent	Incr. or decr. White Amount	Incr. or decr. White Percent	Incr. or decr. Negro Amount	Incr. or decr. Negro Percent
	2	3	4	5	6	7	8	9	10	11	12	13
Alabama	$16,445.82	86.9	$2,484.40	13.1	$16,869.02	79.8	$4,270.42	20.2	$423.20	2.6	$1,786.02	71.9
Arkansas	10,476.20	100.0			14,241.72	98.3	250.00	1.7	3,765.52	35.7	250.00	100.0
Delaware	5,987.50	100.0			6,566.67	100.0			579.17	9.7		
Florida	4,555.08	93.8	300.00	6.2	10,558.15	94.0	675.00	6.0	6,003.07	131.8	375.00	125.0
Georgia	17,361.50	94.8	950.00	5.2	12,786.19	93.9	837.00	6.1	-4,575.31	-26.3	-113.00	-11.9
Kentucky	11,681.01	100.0			12,023.84	91.3	1,139.87	8.7	342.83	2.9	1,139.87	100.0
Louisiana	15,684.23	86.7	2,400.00	13.3	12,926.19	80.0	3,169.31	19.7	-2,758.04	-17.6	769.31	32.1
Maryland	9,201.26	100.0			8,037.02	100.0			-1,164.24	-12.7		
Mississippi	9,694.45	82.9	1,996.68	17.1	8,589.87	83.5	1,691.53	16.5	-1,104.58	-11.4	-305.15	-15.3
Missouri	18,326.32	100.0			13,789.29	100.0			-4,537.03	-24.8		
New Jersey	26,483.67	100.0			22,844.69	100.0			-3,638.98	-13.7		
North Carolina	7,259.29	71.3	2,922.79	28.7	9,359.75	74.7	3,163.25	25.3	2,100.46	28.9	240.46	8.2
Oklahoma	18,242.92	94.7	1,020.36	5.3	17,952.51	94.2	1,095.55	5.8	-290.41	-1.6	75.19	7.4
South Carolina	6,161.04	67.8	2,925.00	32.2	12,418.93	84.4	2,299.65	15.6	6,257.89	101.5	-625.35	-21.4
Tennessee	14,594.94	100.0			12,167.82	90.7	1,245.00	9.3	-2,427.12	-16.6	1,245.00	100.0
Texas	23,172.25	81.4	5,288.02	18.6	25,465.87	84.7	4,602.18	15.3	2,293.62	9.9	-685.84	-12.9
Virginia	10,816.78	82.6	2,281.25	17.4	12,290.63	84.8	2,210.25	15.2	1,473.85	13.6	-71.00	-3.1
West Virginia	11,322.90	96.6	393.75	3.4	2,509.60	83.4	500.00	16.6	-8,813.30	-77.8	106.25	27.0
Total	237,467.16	91.2	22,962.25	8.8	231,397.76	89.5	27,149.01	10.5	-6,069.40	-2.5	4,186.76	18.2

CHARACTERISTICS OF REPRESENTATIVE VOCATIONAL COURSES

Information concerning the period during which courses were offered, grade in which offered, time allotted to laboratory and shop work and to group discussion, condition on which offered, requirements, and criteria in marking was sought from high schools and colleges. Data were received from 863 teachers as follows: 48 of agriculture, 325 of home economics, 385 of industrial arts, and 105 of commercial subjects. Those reporting from Southern high schools numbered 397, from Northern high schools, 367, and from Negro colleges, 99.

Period during which courses are offered.—Eighty-nine percent of the high school, and 59 percent of the college teachers indicated that courses were 1-year courses and were offered each year. The percentages of the high-school and college teachers offering semester courses were 6.4 and 36.4, respectively. There are very slight differences among the subject-matter fields in the percentages of high-school teachers teaching year and semester courses. In the colleges the following percentages of the teachers offered year courses: Agriculture, 71; home economics, 45; trades and industries, 62. Few courses were offered in alternate years, or only when elected by students in either high schools or colleges.

A large proportion of the high-school teachers offered agricultural courses in the seventh and eighth grades; a smaller proportion offered courses in home economics and trades and industries in these grades; and practically none of the commercial teachers offered courses in the seventh and eighth grades. The percentages of the teachers of different subjects offering courses in the seventh and eighth grades follow:

| | Percent offering courses in— | |
Kind of teachers	Seventh grade	Eighth grade
Agriculture	62.5	84.3
Home economics	25.5	40.3
Trades and industries	16.4	27.0

Emphasis on various aspects of courses.—When the number of courses in the different fields are combined, it is found that a majority of the teachers devoted three-fourths of the class time to activities in the shop, laboratory, and garden, and one-fourth to group discussion (see table 43). When agriculture is considered separately it is found that a majority devoted 50 percent or less time to laboratory or shop work. Detailed data are given in the table.

Condition on which courses are offered.—Certain vocational courses are required of some students and are elective for others (see table 44) while a few are required of and others are elective for all students. Eighteen high-school teachers of agriculture and 124 teachers of industrial arts reported that courses were required of all boys.

TABLE 43.—*Number of teachers indicating the percentage of the total time allotted to practical work [1] and to discussion*

Percent of time allotted	High schools					Colleges				
	Agri-culture	Home eco-nomics	Indus-trial arts	Com-mer-cial studies	Total	Agri-culture	Home eco-nomics	Indus-trial arts	Com-mer-cial studies	Total
1	2	3	4	5	6	7	8	9	10	11
To practical work:										
10	2	4	10	6	22	1	1	2	------	4
25	12	25	21	10	68	4	4	1	------	9
50	11	82	67	20	180	9	10	3	1	23
75	7	152	198	28	385	1	18	25	2	46
100	------	14	32	15	61	------	1	8	------	9
Total	32	277	328	79	716	15	34	39	3	91
To group discussion:										
10	4	37	95	22	158	------	------	5	------	5
25	13	157	196	32	398	1	18	16	2	37
50	10	65	21	17	113	9	11	9	------	29
75	5	16	6	8	35	4	4	------	1	9
100	------	2	2	5	9	1	1	5	------	7
Total	32	277	320	84	713	15	34	35	3	87

[1] Practical work as used here means shop, laboratory, garden projects, etc.

TABLE 44.—*Number of teachers indicating condition on which courses are offered*

Condition on which courses are offered	High schools				Colleges			
	Agri-culture	Home eco-nomics	Indus-trial arts	Com-mer-cial studies	Agri-culture	Home eco-nomics	Indus-trial arts	Com-mer-cial studies
1	2	3	4	5	6	7	8	9
Required of boys only	18	------	124	------	5	------	14	------
Required of all students	------	19	8	12	1	1	10	------
Required of all vocational students	2	15	19	5	6	2	8	------
Required of those majoring in department	3	59	88	53	13	30	36	3
Elective for all students	1	55	29	22	1	12	13	3
Elective for boys only	6	4	66	1	2	------	1	------
Elective for vocational students only	------	6	16	1	1	------	------	------
Elective for those majoring in department	------	5	7	2	------	1	1	------
Required of all girls	------	82	------	------	------	------	------	------
Elective for girls	------	5	------	------	------	------	------	------

Manner of conducting classes.—Information was collected concerning the manner of conducting vocational classes for Negroes on the following: Types of materials used (table 45); criteria in determining marks (table 46); freedom permitted in choice of projects (table 47); and required work in related subjects. Textbooks and notebooks were used by a higher percentage of the teachers (70) than other types of materials. "Quality of product" was the criterion considered for determining marks by the highest percentage of teachers; "laboratory exercises" was next. Sixty-three and forty-six percent, respectively, of the high-school and college teachers allowed students to choose the shop, laboratory, or field project.

TABLE 45.—*Number of teachers indicating types of materials used in conduct of courses*

Types of materials used or required	High schools					Colleges				
	Agri-culture	Home eco-nomics	Indus-trial arts	Com-mer-cial studies	Total	Agri-culture	Home eco-nomics	Indus-trial arts	Com-mer-cial studies	Total
1	2	3	4	5	6	7	8	9	10	11
Textbook	24	173	205	93	495	14	23	29	3	69
References	29	173	237	46	485	15	28	35	2	80
Term paper	6	62	50	11	129	9	18	4	------	31
Syllabus	4	6	24	6	40	5	7	3	------	15
Dictation	10	97	107	65	279	2	6	2	2	12
Mimeographed material	10	90	141	53	294	------	12	7	------	19
Notebook	27	220	192	55	494	10	18	20	1	49
Total number of teachers replying	28	270	314	96	708	16	27	37	1	81

TABLE 46.—*Number of teachers indicating the criteria given most weight in determining students' marks*

Criteria	High schools					Colleges				
	Agri-culture	Home eco-nomics	Indus-trial arts	Com-mer-cial studies	Total	Agri-culture	Home eco-nomics	Indus-trial arts	Com-mer-cial studies	Total
1	2	3	4	5	6	7	8	9	10	11
Participation in class and discussion	6	23	6	6	41	5	5	------	------	10
General attitude toward work	7	44	49	6	106	------	1	2	------	3
Final examination	2	12	17	14	45	7	4	7	1	19
Oral quizzes	1	3	1	1	6	------	------	1	------	1
Daily recitation responses	3	16	11	8	38	2	------	1	1	4
Series of examinations	1	5	16	12	34	2	1	4	------	7
Term papers	------	1	------	------	1	------	1	1	------	2
Written papers or projects	6	12	27	7	52	------	1	1	------	2
Laboratory exercises	5	62	69	20	156	1	5	20	2	28
Teachers' judgment of student's work	3	27	47	10	87	------	------	2	------	2
Regular attendance	2	8	6	1	17	------	------	1	------	1
Quality of product	5	62	92	17	176	1	2	3	1	7
Total number of teachers replying	27	194	294	74	546	11	15	31	3	60

TABLE 47.—*Number of vocational teachers of Negroes indicating freedom permitted students in choosing shop or field projects*

Criteria	High schools					Colleges				
	Agriculture	Home economics	Industrial arts	Commercial studies	Total	Agriculture	Home economics	Industrial arts	Commercial studies	Total
1	2	3	4	5	6	7	8	9	10	11
Permitted choice of project_	32	163	209	15	419	7	18	14	1	40
Permitted choice after completing assigned work___	-------	14	20	2	36	1	------	------	------	1
Not permitted to choose project_____	-------	100	99	63	262	6	14	24	2	46
Total_____	32	277	328	80	717	14	32	38	3	87

CONCLUSIONS

According to the findings presented in this chapter, many of the teachers of Negroes in the vocations are inadequately prepared. About half of the teachers in public high schools were college graduates. Approximately a fourth had 2 years or less of college education. Forty-nine had 4 years or less of high-school education. While this number is relatively small, the handicaps which their inadequate preparation places upon the pupils they teach may result in serious consequences for the individuals concerned. The fact that teachers with the most experience have the least education is indicative of a lack of progressiveness. Teachers with inadequate education cannot be expected to develop in pupils that capacity for adjustment required of workers today.

Salaries in rural areas are generally lower than those in urban centers, which may account for the relatively low salaries received by teachers of agriculture. There was considerable difference in the median annual salaries of vocational teachers of Negroes between the Northern and Western and the Southern regions, although the difference in training was slight. The difference in salary may be partially accounted for by the fact that a larger proportion in the Southern region than in the Northern and Western regions are teachers of agriculture, and probably are in rural or small communities.

The fact that a large percentage of the teachers offered vocational courses in the seventh and eighth grades is important because a large number of Negro pupils drop out before they reach high school, where most of the vocational courses are offered. Because of the value to pupils of working on projects in which they are interested, they should be allowed a reasonable amount of freedom, under guidance, in choosing projects. A large percent of the teachers studied did not permit pupils to choose the project on which they were to work.

CHAPTER VIII

Information Needed for Guidance

KNOWLEDGE of pupils is an important factor in guidance. Information concerning the social and economic backgrounds, interests, and school activities, and achievement and progress of pupils is essential in effective educational and vocational guidance. This chapter of the report is an attempt to supply such information.

The data are from 27,980 pupils in 33 States and the District of Columbia.

SOCIAL AND ECONOMIC BACKGROUND

The occupation and education of parents indicate roughly the economic and cultural background of the pupils. Information concerning them is valuable in understanding their possible influence on the pupils' educational and vocational choices and in predicting the probabilities of continuing through high school. Data in tables 48, 49, and 50 represent the type of information which schools should have about each pupil. Facts relating to conditions of the homes from which children come are also of definite help in guidance and counseling. Principals of high schools and university specialists in secondary education ranked home condition second in importance for guidance purposes in a list of 18 items concerned with pupils

TABLE 48.—*Number and percent of Negro high-school pupils whose fathers are engaged in given occupation*

Father's occupation	Pupils	
	Number	*Percent*
Agriculture	1, 464	7. 3
Forestry and fishing	72	. 4
Extraction of minerals	171	. 9
Manufacturing and mechanical industries	5, 335	26. 6
Transportation and communication	1, 710	8. 5
Trade	1, 032	5. 1
Public service	1, 352	6. 7
Professional service	1, 204	6. 0
Semiprofessional service	38	. 2
Domestic and personal service	3, 771	18. 8
Clerical occupations	409	2. 0
Other	3, 505	17. 5
Total	20, 063	100.0

77

background appearing on 249 permanent record cards.[1]   The kind of home and its upkeep, the opportunities for study and healthful sleep and recreation, the quality and number of books, magazines, and newspapers available have a bearing on the pupil's ability to profit by the educational program provided.   Tables 51 and 52 are presented here merely to illustrate the types of data valuable to teachers and counselors.   Their chief value is in their application to individual pupils.

TABLE 49.—*Median years of education attained by parents of pupils, by regions*

	Fathers of—				Mothers of—			
Region	Male students		Female students		Male students		Female students	
	Number of cases	Median	Number of cases	Median	Number of cases	Median	Number of cases	Median
1	2	3	4	5	6	7	8	9
South Atlantic	1,789	8.30	2,561	9.10	1,688	9.26	2,980	8.47
South Central	1,229	8.24	2,024	8.0	1,139	8.37	2,005	8.33
Southwestern	1,414	8.40	2,184	8.3	1,663	8.39	2,969	8.39
Northern and Western	2,457	9.24	3,747	9.02	3,193	9.06	4,364	9.09

TABLE 50.—*Percent of pupils whose fathers and mothers had attained a given educational level*

	South Atlantic		South Central		Southwestern		Northern and Western	
Grade level attained	Fathers	Mothers	Fathers	Mothers	Fathers	Mothers	Fathers	Mothers
1	2	3	4	5	6	7	8	9
	MALE							
Less than seventh grade	29.5	18.2	29.7	23.1	24.7	24.0	20.6	16.2
Seventh grade	11.7	12.9	11.1	12.0	9.1	12.3	8.0	11.4
Eighth grade	11.0	13.8	17.2	19.1	17.6	16.8	19.8	20.3
1 year of high school	7.1	7.7	8.6	10.6	8.2	8.7	10.0	11.8
2 years of high school	5.2	6.4	5.0	5.0	7.4	7.2	8.0	8.8
3 years of high school	3.9	6.0	4.6	5.1	5.1	6.2	5.5	6.5
4 years of high school	10.7	13.5	8.5	9.4	10.7	10.1	12.1	10.9
1 year of college	2.8	3.4	3.8	3.3	3.5	3.8	3.1	3.9
2 years of college	2.8	4.7	2.9	5.3	3.1	2.3	2.9	2.9
3 years of college	2.0	2.7	1.9	1.6	1.9	1.9	2.5	2.2
4 years of college	9.9	8.8	5.0	5.3	7.1	6.1	6.3	3.8
Other	3.3	1.9	1.8	.4	1.6	.4	1.2	1.4
	FEMALE							
Less than seventh grade	19.2	20.7	34.3	24.1	26.7	21.9	20.9	16.7
Seventh grade	11.1	14.4	12.3	13.5	10.8	13.1	8.7	10.4
Eighth grade	13.9	15.4	18.9	18.4	16.0	18.8	18.9	19.8
1 year of high school	12.5	8.7	2.6	8.7	9.1	8.1	10.2	12.7
2 years of high school	5.7	6.2	4.1	6.4	6.6	9.3	6.9	8.3
3 years of high school	5.7	6.3	4.1	5.1	7.2	5.6	5.5	5.8
4 years of high school	11.8	11.7	8.2	9.5	9.1	9.3	13.2	12.0
1 year of college	3.4	3.1	3.0	3.3	2.9	3.3	3.4	4.4
2 years of college	3.0	3.5	2.9	4.3	3.5	3.6	3.2	3.0
3 years of college	1.4	3.0	1.9	2.3	2.0	1.7	1.9	1.6
4 years of college	9.9	6.2	6.6	4.3	4.8	4.7	5.3	3.7
Other	2.4	.8	1.1		1.3	.5	1.9	1.9

[1] Koos, L. V., *and* Kefauver, G. N.   Guidance in Secondary Schools.   New York City, The Macmillan Co., 1932, p. 239.

Information about parents.—Information concerning the occupations of fathers was obtained from 20,063 pupils included in this survey as shown in table 48.   The fathers of 6.2 percent of the pupils reporting were engaged in professional and semiprofessional occupations, showing a situation different from average since 2.5 percent of the total gainfully employed Negroes are professional workers.

According to findings in this study, a larger percentage of the children whose fathers are engaged in the professional, trade, and clerical occupations attained a higher level of education than others.   For the males the respective percentages are 63, 65, and 62; for the females, 69, 69, and 72. There is no evidence that the father's occupation influenced the grade level at which the high-school nongraduates left school.   Information concerning the education of parents is given in tables 49 and 50.

Home status of pupils.—Slightly more than one-third (36 percent) of the parents of pupils included in this study owned or were buying their homes. The corresponding percentage for the Negro population as a whole, according to the 1930 census, was 23.9.   The median number of rooms in the homes of the pupils was 5.95; and the median number of persons in the homes was 6.05.   The percentages of the homes having given conveniences were: Electricity, 78; bathtub, 61.5; toilet, 73.8; piano, 47; and radio, 68.

Three-fourths of the pupils come from homes possessing 100 or fewer books (table 51).   Seven percent subscribed to no newspaper (table 52). Another 8 percent did not subscribe to a daily paper, but did subscribe to a Negro paper.   A total of 30 percent did not subscribe to a Negro paper.

TABLE 51.—*Number and percent of pupils indicating the number of books in home*

Number of books	Region									
	Southwestern		South Atlantic		South Central		Northern and Western		Total	
	Number	Percent	Number	Percent	Number	Percent	Number	Percent	Number	Percent
1	2	3	4	5	6	7	8	9	10	11
25 or fewer	1,924	38.2	1,743	25.5	1,479	32.4	2,761	27.9	7,907	30.1
26 to 100	2,195	43.5	3,177	46.6	2,022	44.2	4,701	47.5	12,095	45.9
101 to 500	809	16.0	1,585	23.2	889	19.4	2,113	21.3	5,396	20.4
501 to 1,000	90	1.8	238	3.5	147	3.2	224	2.3	699	2.7
1,000 or more	25	.5	81	1.2	37	.8	106	1.0	249	.9
Total	5,043	100.0	6,824	100.0	4,574	100.0	9,905	100.0	26,346	100.0
Median number of books per home	46.42	------	65.43	------	74.51	------	61.28	------	59.65	------

TABLE 52.—*Number and percent of pupils from homes subscribing and not subscribing to newspapers*

Newspapers	Region									
	Southwestern		South Atlantic		South Central		Northern and Western		Total	
	Number	Percent	Number	Percent	Number	Percent	Number	Percent	Number	Percent
1	2	3	4	5	6	7	8	9	10	11
No daily and no Negro	445	8.63	492	7.35	386	8.45	608	6.12	1,931	7.30
No daily and one or more Negro	575	11.11	532	7.94	374	8.19	611	6.16	2,092	7.94
One or more daily and no Negro	932	18.04	1,491	22.26	1,274	27.91	2,235	22.52	5,932	22.51
One or more daily and one or more Negro	3,214	62.22	4,183	62.45	2,529	55.41	6,466	65.19	16,392	62.21
Other					1	.02	2	.02	3	.01
Total	5,166	100.0	6,698	100.0	4,564	100.0	9,922	100.0	26,350	100.0

SCHOOL INTERESTS, ACTIVITIES, AND ACHIEVEMENTS

Information concerning school interests, activities, and progress oʃ pupils is of value to teachers and counselors in furnishing guidance. Extraclassroom activities provide try-out and exploratory possibilities; develop initiative, leadership, and independence; broaden interests; and assist in discovering capacities. Self-support of pupils furnishes opportunity to gain practical experience, to develop certain habits required in the occupational world, such as industry, perseverance, punctuality, and independence. Self-support is detrimental when the amount and condition of the work interferes with the educational program, or is injurious to the pupils' health or character. Information concerning acceleration and retardation has a bearing on possible withdrawal, failure, and success of pupils. (See tables 53, 54, and 55.) Table 53 shows the extracurriculum activities of this group of students and indicates acceptable types of such activities. Table 54 establishes norms for use by counselors, and also shows the large number of pupils overage, as does table 55. These data indicate that the high-school curriculum probably needs adjustment and better articulation with the elementary school.

Extra-classroom activities and self-support.—Information was gathered from 22,562 pupils concerning participation in certain extra-classroom activities (table 53). The largest percentage of pupils engaged in the activities listed was in athletic teams and squads. Home-room and class organization, in which 35.5 and 28.5 percent of the pupils, respectively, participated, are frequently required and therefore are not comparable to the other activities. However, they are important as indicating the proportion of the pupils who participate in them.

According to information obtained from 27,980 pupils, approximately two-thirds supported themselves in part or entirely; 47 percent, in part; 17.3 percent entirely.

TABLE 53.—*Percentage of pupils who participated in certain extra-classroom activities*

Activity	Percent	Activity	Percent
Student council	12. 2	Debating society	2. 6
Class organization	28. 5	School honor society	3. 9
Home room	35. 5	4–H clubs	2. 4
Musical organization	14. 6	Future farmers	. 8
School publications	3. 6	Boy Scouts	. 08
Athletic teams or squads	24. 2	Girl Reserves	. 6
Dramatic clubs	8. 3	High Y	. 1
Other school organizations	19. 4	Other	3. 1
Fraternities, sororities, social	6. 3	None	2. 7
Traffic or safety squads	6. 9		

School progress.—The percentages of children entering first-year high school at given ages are shown in table 54. Approximately three-fourths, or 72.1 percent, were 14 years of age and above. One-third were 15 or 16 years of age. A smaller percentage in the Northern and a larger percentage in the South Atlantic than in the other regions entered when relatively young.

Of the 27,366 pupils reported, one-third were overage for their grade. This is an improvement over the situation found among Negro high-school pupils in rural areas in a former study.[2] The percentages of pupils overage in each of the high-school grades in these two studies are as follows:

Study	Grade				
	Eighth	Ninth	Tenth	Eleventh	Twelfth
1	2	3	4	5	6
	Percent	*Percent*	*Percent*	*Percent*	*Percent*
Present	49. 5	34. 8	29. 2	29. 6	25. 2
Former	82. 6	76. 7	72. 3	70. 5	

Details regarding the situation are shown in table 55. In each grade a smaller percentage of girls than boys is overage, as in the other studies. A smaller percentage of the pupils in the Northern and Western regions is overage for grade in which enrolled than in the other regions, as shown in the following: Northern and Western, 29; South Atlantic, 31.2; South Central, 32.9; Southwestern, 40.6. Details concerning the age-grade status of the pupils in the different regions are shown in table 5 in appendix A.

[2] Availability of Education to Negroes in Rural Communities. Op. cit., p. 63.

TABLE 54.—*Number and percent* [1] *of pupils of given age when entered first-year high school* [2]

Age	Southwestern		South Atlantic		South Central		Northern and Western		Total	
	Number	Percent	Number	Percent	Number	Percent	Number	Percent	Number	Percent
1	2	3	4	5	6	7	8	9	10	11
10 years or less	16	0.3	20	0.3	11	0.2	12	0.1	59	0.2
11	98	1.9	160	2.2	43	.9	37	.4	338	1.2
12	450	8.6	761	10.6	299	6.5	437	4.2	1,947	7.1
13	1,131	21.6	1,714	23.8	842	18.3	1,578	15.3	5,265	19.2
14	1,487	28.4	2,147	29.8	1,202	26.1	3,370	32.6	8,206	29.9
15	1,130	21.6	1,410	19.6	1,048	22.8	2,731	26.4	6,319	23.1
16	591	11.3	641	8.9	637	13.8	1,390	13.5	3,259	11.9
17	211	4.0	225	3.1	317	6.9	489	4.7	1,242	4.5
18	86	1.6	83	1.1	122	2.6	204	1.9	495	1.8
19	24	.5	23	.3	46	.9	62	.6	155	.6
20 years or more	9	.2	27	.3	37	.8	18	.2	91	.3
No response	60	------	244	------	161	------	160	------	625	------
Total	5,293	------	7,455	------	4,765	------	10,488	------	28,001	------
Median	14.62	------	14.44	------	14.92	------	14.92	------	14.74	------

[1] Students not responding were deducted from totals in order to compute percentages.
[2] The first year of a 4-year high school, or a 3-year senior high school.

TABLE 55.—*Age-grade distribution of Negro high-school pupils in 33 States and the District of Columbia, 1936–37*

Age	Eighth¹ Male	Eighth¹ Female	Eighth¹ Total	Ninth Male	Ninth Female	Ninth Total	Tenth Male	Tenth Female	Tenth Total	Eleventh Male	Eleventh Female	Eleventh Total	Twelfth Male	Twelfth Female	Twelfth Total	Grand total Male	Grand total Female	Grand total Total
1	2	3	4	5	6	7	8	9	10	11	12	13	14	15	16	17	18	19
14 years or less	539	815	1,354	1,025	1,841	2,866	258	577	835	65	115	180	10	12	22	1,897	3,360	5,257
15	248	376	624	1,008	1,582	2,590	735	1,286	2,021	245	527	772	59	64	123	2,295	3,835	6,130
16	156	229	385	759	946	1,705	812	1,341	2,153	560	1,136	1,696	159	326	485	2,446	3,978	6,424
17	90	99	189	379	371	750	534	684	1,218	572	1,017	1,589	308	642	950	1,883	2,813	4,696
18	59	29	88	137	146	283	244	316	560	410	658	1,068	333	509	842	1,183	1,658	2,841
19	20	6	26	54	40	94	104	84	188	216	226	442	242	259	501	636	615	1,251
20	9	2	11	26	8	34	34	15	49	82	68	150	97	79	176	248	172	420
21	2	-	2	12	6	18	16	5	21	29	24	53	42	35	77	101	70	171
22	-	-	-	4	3	7	5	2	7	14	17	31	20	9	29	43	31	74
23	-	1	1	2	4	6	3	4	7	13	8	21	6	4	10	24	21	45
24 years or more	-	1	1	6	3	9	7	5	12	8	6	14	13	8	21	34	23	57
Total: Number	1,123	1,558	2,681	3,412	4,950	8,362	2,752	4,319	7,071	2,214	3,802	6,016	1,289	1,947	3,236	10,790	16,576	27,366
Percent	10.4	9.3	9.8	31.6	29.9	30.6	25.5	26.1	25.8	20.5	22.9	22.0	12.0	11.7	11.8	100.0	100.0	100.0
Normal: Number	539	815	1,354	2,033	3,423	5,456	1,547	2,627	4,174	1,132	2,153	3,285	641	1,151	1,792	5,892	10,169	16,061
Percent	48.0	52.3	50.5	59.6	69.2	65.2	56.2	60.8	59.0	51.1	56.6	54.6	49.7	59.1	55.4	54.6	61.3	58.7
Overage: Number	584	743	1,327	1,379	1,527	2,906	947	1,115	2,062	772	1,007	1,779	420	394	814	4,102	4,786	8,888
Percent	52.0	47.7	49.5	40.4	30.8	34.8	34.4	25.8	29.2	34.8	26.5	29.6	32.6	20.2	25.2	38.0	28.9	32.5
Underage: Number	-	-	-	-	-	-	258	577	835	310	642	952	228	402	630	796	1,621	2,417
Percent	-	-	-	-	-	-	9.4	13.4	11.8	14.0	16.9	15.8	17.7	20.6	19.5	7.4	9.8	8.8

¹ In several States in the South where the elementary schools consist of 7 grades, the eighth grade constitutes the first year of high school.

PUPILS' OCCUPATIONAL CHOICES

The choice of an occupation is one of the vital decisions which every normal individual must make; for this reason both teachers and counselors should have as much information as possible which will help in making an intelligent selection. While the choices which pupils make are not always final, they frequently have an influence on their curriculum choices and on the length of time they stay in school. Of the many possible influences on occupational choice the following are discussed here: Geographical region (table 56), age and educational advancement, size of community (table 57), personal motives or influences (table 58), hobbies or interests (table 59), and occupation and education of parents (table 60).

From the standpoint of guidance it is important to know what influence, if any, age of pupils and grade level in high school have on occupational choice and what variation in choice may be expected in different geographical regions. Information concerning influences in choosing an occupation should be helpful in assisting pupils in developing different motives or in changing occupational objectives, when desirable. Information about interests may assist in revealing educational and occupational interests, and may lead to the discovery of capacity in particular activities. A study of pupils' choice of occupation in relation to parents' occupations and education may aid in the discovery of motives for occupational choice and may indicate the possible future contentment in the occupation chosen.

Occupational choice in the different regions.—A comparison of the occupational choice of pupils, by sex, in the different geographical regions is shown in table 56. Among the males there appear to be significant differences among the regions in the percentages choosing occupations in manufacturing and mechanical industries, public service, professional service, and clerical service. Among the females, differences are in manufacturing and mechanical industries, professional service, and clerical service.

The distribution of pupils making certain occupational choices according to the size of the communities in which the schools are located is shown in table 57. A larger percentage of the males in the small communities than in the large ones chose agriculture. In manufacturing and mechanical industries the differences are very slight with the exception of communities of 50,000 to 99,999 population. The percentage of females choosing occupations of this kind increases consistently with the size of the community. A smaller percentage of both males and females in communities of 100,000 or more, than in the smaller communities, choose professional service, the difference being greater among the females. There is also a difference between the small and large communities in the percentage of females choosing clerical occupations.

Occupational choice by age and educational advancement.—According to data received from 5,517 high-school boys and 9,350 high-school girls, age has little influence on choice of occupation.

TABLE 56.—*Number and percent of pupils indicating occupational choice, by sex and region*

Agriculture

Region	Male Number	Male Percent	Female Number	Female Percent	Total Number	Total Percent
1	2	3	4	5	6	7
Southwest	37	2.2	-----	-----	37	0.8
South Atlantic	46	2.2	1	0.02	47	.8
South Central	25	1.9	-----	-----	25	.7
Northern and Western	13	.4	-----	-----	13	.1
Total	121	1.4	1	.1	122	.6

Manufacturing and mechanical industries

Region	Male Number	Male Percent	Female Number	Female Percent	Total Number	Total Percent
1	8	9	10	11	12	13
Southwest	281	16.7	128	4.3	409	8.8
South Atlantic	542	25.8	142	4.0	684	12.2
South Central	215	16.2	101	4.1	316	8.3
Northern and Western	795	24.8	500	9.8	1,295	15.6
Total	1,833	22.0	871	6.2	2,704	12.1

Transportation and communication

Region	Male Number	Male Percent	Female Number	Female Percent	Total Number	Total Percent
1	14	15	16	17	18	19
Southwest	46	2.7	2	0.06	48	1.03
South Atlantic	49	2.3	1	.02	50	.9
South Central	52	3.9	-----	.04	53	1.4
Northern and Western	70	2.2	10	.2	80	.9
Total	217	2.6	14	.1	231	1.0

Trade

Region	Male Number	Male Percent	Female Number	Female Percent	Total Number	Total Percent
Southwest	84	5.0	9	0.3	93	2.0
South Atlantic	145	7.0	42	1.2	187	3.3
South Central	94	7.1	27	1.1	121	3.2
Northern and Western	185	5.8	80	1.5	265	3.2
Total	508	6.1	158	1.1	666	3.0

Public service

Region	Male Number	Male Percent	Female Number	Female Percent	Total Number	Total Percent
Southwest	243	14.5	3	0.1	246	5.3
South Atlantic	175	8.3	9	.2	184	3.3
South Central	162	12.2	-----	-----	162	4.3
Northern and Western	295	9.2	19	.4	314	3.8
Total	875	10.5	31	.2	906	4.0

Professional service

Region	Male Number	Male Percent	Female Number	Female Percent	Total Number	Total Percent
Southwest	874	52.1	2,178	74.0	3,052	65.9
South Atlantic	983	47.9	2,681	76.1	3,664	65.2
South Central	664	49.9	1,842	74.7	2,506	66.1
Northern and Western	1,437	44.7	2,926	57.4	4,363	52.5
Total	3,958	47.6	9,627	68.6	13,585	60.8

Semiprofessional

Region	Male Number	Male Percent	Female Number	Female Percent	Total Number	Total Percent
Southwest	3	0.2	6	0.2	9	0.2
South Atlantic	6	.3	8	-----	14	.2
South Central	7	.5	5	.2	12	.3
Northern and Western	46	1.4	37	.7	83	1.0
Total	62	.7	56	.4	118	.5

Domestic and personal service

Region	Male Number	Male Percent	Female Number	Female Percent	Total Number	Total Percent
Southwest	37	2.2	199	6.7	236	5.1
South Atlantic	41	2.0	180	5.1	221	3.9
South Central	12	.9	155	6.3	167	4.4
Northern and Western	35	1.1	339	6.6	374	4.5
Total	125	1.5	873	6.2	998	4.5

Clerical

Region	Male Number	Male Percent	Female Number	Female Percent	Total Number	Total Percent
Southwest	42	2.5	400	13.6	442	9.6
South Atlantic	82	3.9	389	11.0	471	8.4
South Central	79	5.9	324	13.1	403	10.6
Northern and Western	228	7.1	1,094	21.5	1,322	15.9
Total	431	5.2	2,207	15.7	2,638	11.8

Other

Region	Male Number	Male Percent	Female Number	Female Percent	Total Number	Total Percent
Southwest	32	1.9	24	0.8	56	1.2
South Atlantic	25	1.2	71	2.0	96	1.7
South Central	20	1.5	8	.3	28	.7
Northern and Western	106	3.3	95	1.9	201	2.4
Total	183	2.2	198	1.4	381	1.7

Total

Region	Male Number	Female Number	Total Number
Southwest	1,679	2,949	4,628
South Atlantic	2,094	3,524	5,618
South Central	1,330	2,463	3,793
Northern and Western	3,210	5,100	8,310
Total	8,313	14,036	22,349

In order to find whether or not grade level of pupils has any influence on occupational choice the percentages of pupils in each grade selecting occupations in the manufacturing and mechanical industries and professional service were computed as samples. The percentages selecting manufacturing and mechanical industries for each high-school grade follow: First year, 22.7; second year, 21.2; third year, 17.5; and fourth year, 14.2. The percentages in each grade choosing professional occupations were: First year, 67; second year, 63; third year, 64; and fourth year, 66. Although the percentages for all the occupations were not computed, judging from the above, it appears that grade level has no marked influence on the occupational choice of Negro high-school pupils. This conclusion, if supported by further study, would seem to indicate the need of a closer relation between curriculums and courses, and vocational interests of pupils.

TABLE 57.—*Number and percent of pupils indicating choice of occupation, by size of community*

Students' choice of occupation	Size of community									
	Fewer than 2,500		2,500–49,999		50,000 –99,999		100,000 and more		Total	
	Number	Percent	Number	Percent	Number	Percent	Number	Percent	Number	Percent
1	2	3	4	5	6	7	8	9	10	11
Agriculture:										
Male	16	6.8	41	4.5	7	1.5	20	0.4	84	1.2
Female			1						1	
Forestry and fishing:										
Male							2	.03	2	.02
Female										
Extraction of minerals:										
Male							3	.05	3	.04
Female							1		1	
Manufacturing and mechanical industries:										
Male	50	21.4	180	19.7	74	15.4	1,332	23.9	1,636	22.7
Female	8	2.3	47	2.9	50	5.9	646	7.0	751	6.3
Transportation and communication:										
Male	5	2.1	20	2.2	20	4.2	138	2.5	183	2.5
Female			1				11	.1	13	.1
Trade:										
Male	20	8.5	63	6.9	33	6.9	282	5.1	398	5.5
Female	1	.3	18	1.1	9	1.1	154	1.7	182	1.5
Public service:										
Male	8	3.4	72	7.9	54	11.3	671	12.0	805	11.2
Female			9	.6	5	.6	175	1.9	189	1.6
Professional service:										
Male	120	51.3	453	49.6	251	52.4	2,316	41.6	3,140	43.6
Female	286	83.4	1,250	78.2	620	73.9	5,679	61.7	7,835	65.3
Semiprofessional:										
Male	1	.4	2	.2			64	1.1	67	.9
Female			4	.3	1	.1	50	.5	55	.5
Domestic and personal service:										
Male	5	2.1	27	2.9	15	3.1	56	1.0	103	1.4
Female	13	3.8	107	6.7	45	5.4	534	5.8	699	5.8
Clerical occupations:										
Male	7	2.9	33	3.6	10	2.1	263	4.7	313	4.3
Female	23	6.7	132	3.2	85	10.1	1,574	17.1	1,814	15.1
Other:										
Male	2	.9	23	2.5	15	3.1	425	7.6	465	6.5
Female	12	3.5	30	1.8	23	2.7	378	4.1	443	3.7
Total:										
Male	234	40.6	914	36.4	479	36.3	5,572	37.7	7,199	37.8
Female	343	59.4	1,599	63.6	839	63.7	9,202	62.3	11,983	62.2

Influences in choosing an occupation.—The influences which pupils said affected the selection of an occupation are shown in table 58. Three influences predominate in all the regions among both boys and girls, namely, "desire to make money," "belief in ability in special field," and "desire to serve."

Choice of occupation, according to interest.—Data concerning hobbies or interests and occupational choice are shown in table 59. Of the 363 male pupils whose hobby was scientific and mechanical construction, 37.5 percent gave manufacturing and mechanical industries as their occupational choice; while 6.6 percent chose transportation and communication service. Both of these occupations have rather close relation to the hobby. Of the 991 male pupils whose hobby was home workshop or laboratory, 29 percent chose manufacturing and mechanical industries as an occupation. Further analysis of the data may be made by those interested in order to study any possible relationship between other hobbies and occupational choice.

Choice of occupation, according to father's occupation.—The extent to which Negro high-school pupils choose the vocations in which their fathers are engaged was studied. In the South Atlantic region 4 percent of the girls chose occupations in manufacturing and mechanical industries, while 20 percent of the girls' fathers were engaged in these occupations. Fathers of 2.5 percent of the girls were engaged in clerical occupations, but 10.6 percent chose these occupations. Three-fourths of the girls chose professional service, while only one-twentieth of their fathers were so engaged.

In the South Atlantic region, 20.7 percent of the boys' fathers were engaged in manufacturing and mechanical industries, and 25.3 percent of the boys expressed a desire to enter these occupations. Two and seventenths percent of the fathers were engaged in clerical service, while 4.6 percent of the sons indicated a preference for clerical work. Nearly half of the boys (47.5 percent) chose the professions, but only 7.7 percent of their fathers were engaged in them. Six and five-tenths percent of the fathers were employed in agriculture, while 1.7 percent of the boys desired to be farmers. In trade occupations there is close agreement between fathers' occupation and sons' choices; the percentages are, respectively, 5.9 and 5.5. The respective percentages of fathers engaged in public service and sons' choices are 14.2 and 9.3. A more exact measure of relationship between occupation of fathers and occupational, choice of their children may be obtained by ascertaining the number of children who expressed a desire to enter the specific occupation in which the fathers are engaged. A total of 203, or 15.7 percent of the male pupils in the South Atlantic region chose the occupation in which their fathers were engaged. The percentage of sons who chose the occupation in which their fathers were engaged for the other regions are: South Central, 17.4; Southwest, 13.2; and Northern, 13.8. A further study of possible relationship between occupations of fathers and occupations engaged in by their sons is reported in chapter 9.

TABLE 58.—*Percent of pupils attributing their choice of occupation to indicated influences, by region and sex*

Influence	South Atlantic		South Central		Southwest		Northern and Western	
	Male	Female	Male	Female	Male	Female	Male	Female
1	2	3	4	5	6	7	8	9
Desire to make money	34.9	28.1	36.5	27.7	39.7	31.5	30.7	27.9
Success of friends	3.3	3.2	4.6	5.7	3.1	3.2	2.3	2.7
Advice of relatives or friends	3.5	2.8	2.7	2.3	4.4	4.8	3.2	2.4
Teachers	2.5	6.1	2.1	8.8	1.6	4.2	1.6	3.8
Desire to serve	13.8	22.1	15.2	18.5	9.9	15.5	10.3	14.8
Advice of parents	5.1	7.2	4.8	6.7	3.8	4.5	6.2	5.8
Observing people at work	3.8	3.0	2.9	2.6	2.4	2.0	3.3	4.3
Working vacations or after school	2.3	.8	.9	1.1	1.3	1.2	1.9	1.1
Things you read	1.2	.8	2.2	.9	2.3	.9	1.4	1.1
Guidance counselor	1.1	.6	.5	.2	.2	.1	1.0	.8
Belief in ability in special field	18.3	20.9	21.9	22.2	23.7	28.2	28.4	30.7
Father's occupation	4.3	.3	2.7	.7	2.8	.4	3.2	1.0
Mother's occupation	.3	.9	.3	1.4	.4	1.6	.1	.8
Course in occupations	.1	.2	.2	.2	.6	.3	.6	.5
Work in shops	3.8	.7	1.8	.4	2.5	.6	3.2	.6
Academic courses in school	.5	1.1	.3	.3	.1	.2	1.3	.9
Extracurricular activities	.3	.2	.1	.04	.2	.2	.2	.1
Motion pictures	.4	.3	.5	.3	.5	.5	.4	.2
Out-of-school activities	.5	.4	.1	.1	.4	.2	1.0	.5
Other	.4	.3	.1	.04	.2	.1	------	------

Choice of occupation and parents' education.—Some information concerning the schooling of parents and the occupational choices of pupils was collected for the purpose of discovering whether or not there is any relationship between them (table 60). In general, the data indicate that children of parents who are college graduates are more apt to choose one of the professions or a career in the manufacturing and mechanical industries than those of parents with seventh-grade education only.

TABLE 59.—*Number of pupils choosing given occupations, according to interest of first preference and percent of pupils expressing first preference for given interest*

Hobby of first preference	Agriculture		Manufacturing and mechanical industries		Transportation and communication		Trade		Public service		Professional service		Semi-professional service		Domestic and personal service		Clerical occupations		Other		Total		Percentage of pupils expressing first preference for given interest	
	Males	Females	Males	Females	Males	Females	Males	Females	Males	Females	Males	Females	Males	Females	Males	Females	Males	Females	Males	Females	Males	Females	Males	Females
1	2	3	4	5	6	7	8	9	10	11	12	13	14	15	16	17	18	19	20	21	22	23	24	25
Home workshop or laboratory	23	—	287	65	21	1	60	8	113	2	412	436	23	5	17	65	28	54	7	4	991	640	14.0	5.5
Athletics	51	—	645	175	79	3	190	39	426	17	1,241	1,527	17	13	53	147	127	406	22	15	2,851	2,342	40.4	20.2
Reading	15	—	118	152	14	—	27	35	64	17	334	2,035	10	10	13	134	35	414	5	17	635	2,815	9.0	24.2
Playing musical instrument	2	—	106	76	13	4	47	15	90	8	494	1,019	10	5	8	46	25	183	3	9	798	1,365	11.3	11.8
Painting and drawing	3	—	56	32	11	1	13	8	36	3	228	319	1	—	2	27	16	49	3	8	368	438	5.2	3.8
Singing	3	—	50	71	9	—	20	20	34	9	150	824	2	8	6	79	21	172	3	8	304	1,192	4.3	10.3
School paper	—	—	12	12	1	1	2	—	6	2	31	112	1	—	3	6	13	33	—	8	59	168	.8	1.4
Movies	2	—	69	63	10	1	19	15	43	9	134	493	3	8	3	35	13	163	1	3	296	784	4.2	6.7
Dancing	—	—	62	109	7	7	20	16	33	13	138	935	2	7	4	69	20	269	6	12	292	1,430	4.1	12.3
Scientific or mechanical construction	4	—	136	6	24	1	15	1	31	1	146	80	1	1	1	7	4	5	3	3	363	98	5.1	.8
Dramatics	2	—	11	8	4	—	5	3	5	1	51	221	3	3	1	7	6	38	1	3	84	284	1.2	2.4
Other	—	—	2	4	2	—	—	—	—	—	10	30	—	—	—	—	—	—	6	6	20	55	.3	.5
Total	111	—	1,554	773	195	12	418	162	881	76	3,369	8,031	70	60	110	624	298	1,795	55	78	7,061	11,611		

TABLE 60.—*Number and percent of pupils whose parents have designated education who expressed a desire to enter a given occupation*

Occupational choice	Males								Females							
	Fathers' education				Mothers' education				Fathers' education				Mothers' education			
	Less than seventh grade		4 years of college		Less than seventh grade		4 years of college		Less than seventh grade		4 years of college		Less than seventh grade		4 years of college	
	Number	Percent	Number	Percent	Number	Percent	Number	Percent	Number	Percent	Number	Percent	Number	Percent	Number	Percent
1	**2**	**3**	**4**	**5**	**6**	**7**	**8**	**9**	**10**	**11**	**12**	**13**	**14**	**15**	**16**	**17**
Agriculture	31	1.7	7	1.4	28	1.9	4	0.9							1	0.2
Manufacturing and mechanical	393	22.0	67	13.3	381	25.4	64	14.6	196	7.6	21	3.0	159	6.4	16	2.8
Transportation and communication	48	2.7	14	2.8	34	2.3	19	4.3							2	.3
Trade	155	8.7	34	6.7	80	5.3	31	7.1	47	1.8	8	1.1	21	.8	3	.5
Public service	207	11.6	43	8.5	192	12.8	43	9.8	19	.7	6	.9		.04		
Professional service	790	44.3	313	62.1	657	43.7	257	58.5	1,627	62.7	568	80.7	1,735	69.4	465	80.2
Semiprofessional service	12	.7	4	.6	7	.5	1	.2	15	.6	7	1.0			7	1.2
Domestic and personal service	41	2.3	4	.8	29	1.9	2	.5	208	8.0	23	3.3	179	7.2	12	2.1
Clerical occupations	83	4.6	13	2.6	70	4.7	16	3.6	464	17.9	66	9.4	381	15.5	72	12.4
Other	25	1.4	6	1.2	24	1.6	2	.4	19	.7	4	.6	13	.5	2	.3
Total	1,785		504		1,502		439		2,595		704		2,499		580	

[CHAPTER IX]

Information Helpful in Formulating Guidance Programs

GENERAL CHARACTERISTICS

WHAT HAPPENS to Negroes who graduate from high school and to those who drop out before graduation? What occupational adjustments do they make? What, if any, relation is there between schooling and occupational adjustment? To what extent has the school assisted former pupils in adjustment? What are their interests and in what activities do they engage? What variation, if any, exists among the different geographical regions with respect to these matters? Information concerning these questions, reported in this chapter, should be helpful in formulating guidance programs. The age of persons studied, the amount and kind of education received, and the work experience while in day school should indicate the kind of assistance needed from schools in making further occupational adjustment. Information concerning reasons for leaving day school and for attending evening school, employment since leaving day school, means of obtaining employment, and relationship of son's to father's occupation is related not only to the present needs of adults but also to whatever revision may be made in educational and guidance programs for youth now in school. The kind of information reported in this chapter is needed about each individual in order to provide effective counseling.

Data were collected from 20,260 high-school graduates and nongraduates during 1926 to 1935 in 33 States and the District of Columbia, in communities of different sizes, and from 2,540 persons who were enrolled in evening school.

Age of students.—The median age of graduates when interviewed and of nongraduates, according to the size of community in which they live, is shown in table 61. The nongraduates are slightly younger than the graduates; when the two groups are combined those who live in the large cities are younger than those living in the small communities.

91

TABLE 61.—*Number and median age of Negro high-school graduates and nongraduates, according to size of community in which they live*

Size of community	Male				Female			
	Graduates		Nongraduates		Graduates		Nongraduates	
	Number	Median	Number	Median	Number	Median	Number	Median
Fewer than 2,500	173	24.30	184	23.09	264	23.53	302	22.60
2,500 to 24,999	592	24.29	488	23.05	1,087	23.84	810	22.50
25,000 to 99,999	974	23.60	966	22.39	1,822	23.34	1,573	22.10
100,000 to 499,999	1,605	22.94	1,571	21.90	3,021	22.53	2,020	21.60
500,000 and more	677	22.27	552	20.47	1,343	21.53	809	20.64
Total	4,021	23.27	3,761	21.90	7,537	22.80	5,514	21.83

The median age of persons when they graduated or dropped out varied slightly among the geographic regions. For male graduates the range is from 18.74 years in the North Atlantic to 19.44 years in the South Central region. For males who did not graduate the range is from 17.63 years in the South Atlantic to 18.29 years in the Southwest region. Median age of female graduates ranged from 18.45 in the North Central region to 18.97 in the South Central; of those who dropped out, from 17.37 years in the South Central region to 17.87 years in the Southwest. The median age of all evening-school students was 26.08 years. Evening-school students in the Northern and Western regions are 2.64 years younger than those in the Southern region. Data in table 62 indicate that the older evening-school students left school earlier than the younger ones.

Educational level attained.—The number and percentage of nongraduates who left school at given grades are shown in table 63. Table 64 shows similar information by regions. The difference in attainment between the nongraduates in the Northern and Western regions and the Southern region is fairly pronounced. For example, the percentages of females reaching the tenth grade or higher in the North Central, North Atlantic, and Western regions are, respectively, 79.8, 78.9, and 81.3. The corresponding percentages are 47.6, 27.7, and 45.8, in the South Atlantic, South Central, and Southwest regions, respectively. Similar comparisons can be made between Northern and Western regions on the basis of median years of education attained for both males and females. Detailed analysis of the education of nongraduates according to size of community was not made, however, the original data are shown in table VI in appendix A for anyone interested in making such an analysis.

Differences among the evening-school students in grades reached before leaving school as shown in table 65 are similar to those found among the nongraduates mentioned above.

TABLE 62.—*Number and median age of evening school students who have attained a given level of education*

	Regions			
Level of education	Northern and western		Southern	
	Number	Median age	Number	Median age
1	2	3	4	5
Elementary:				
1	6		2	
2–4	23	37.83	57	36.58
5–6	47	36.25	142	33.15
7–8	215	35.81	321	29.68
High school:				
9–10	280	23.75	294	25.72
11–12	438	21.68	330	24.08
College:				
1–2	94	26.82	58	25.46
3–4	25	24.96	33	27.35
Did not attend	33	25.21	1	

TABLE 63.—*Number and percent of nongraduates who dropped out of school at given grades*

	Male		Female	
Grade on leaving school	Number	Percent	Number	Percent
1	2	3	4	5
Seventh	48	1.3	35	0.7
Eighth	532	14.7	649	12.3
Ninth	1,054	29.2	1,511	28.6
Tenth	1,038	28.8	1,629	30.9
Eleventh	693	19.2	1,063	20.1
Twelfth	246	6.8	389	7.4
Total	3,611	100.0	5,276	100.0

TABLE 64.—*Number and percent of nongraduates, indicating grade reached, by region*

Grade on leaving school	Region													
	South Atlantic		South Central		Southwest		North Central		North Atlantic		West		Total	
	Number	Percent	Number	Percent	Number	Percent	Number	Percent	Number	Percent	Number	Percent	Number	Percent
1	2	3	4	5	6	7	8	9	10	11	12	13	14	15
MALE NONGRADUATES														
Seventh	35	2.4	---	---	2	0.4	---	---	---	---	4	2.2	49	1.3
Eighth	359	24.9	17	2.4	151	28.4	1	0.3	5	2.4	1	.5	532	14.6
Ninth	389	26.9	299	42.2	159	30.0	105	18.8	58	27.9	50	26.9	1,060	29.2
Tenth	353	24.5	238	33.6	135	25.4	203	36.2	60	28.7	60	32.3	1,049	28.9
Eleventh	226	15.8	120	16.9	75	14.1	172	30.7	60	28.7	44	23.6	697	19.2
Twelfth	80	5.5	32	4.5	9	1.7	77	13.7	24	11.5	27	14.5	249	6.8
Total	1,442	100.0	708	100.0	531	100.0	560	100.0	209	100.0	186	100.0	3,636	100.0
Median	9.84		10.15		9.71		10.85		10.66		10.63		10.17	
FEMALE NONGRADUATES														
Seventh	23	1.2	---	---	5	0.5	---	---	---	---	4	1.2	36	0.7
Eighth	383	20.8	27	2.3	239	25.6	2	0.3	2	0.6	1	.3	655	12.3
Ninth	561	30.4	441	37.1	262	28.1	141	19.2	62	20.5	58	17.2	1,525	28.6
Tenth	465	25.3	391	32.9	269	28.8	285	38.8	108	35.8	125	37.0	1,643	30.8
Eleventh	310	16.8	241	20.3	146	15.6	191	26.0	82	27.2	112	33.1	1,082	20.2
Twelfth	101	5.5	87	7.3	13	1.4	110	15.0	48	15.9	38	11.2	397	7.4
Total	1,843	100.0	1,187	100.0	934	100.0	734	100.0	302	100.0	338	100.0	5,338	100.0
Median	9.92		10.32		9.66		10.77		10.81		10.85		10.04	

TABLE 65.—*Number of evening-school students who left school at stated grade levels, by sex*

Grade level on leaving	Male	Female	Total
1	2	3	4
Elementary:			
1	5	3	8
2–4	40	43	83
5–6	72	127	199
7–8	165	385	550
High school:			
9–10	180	398	578
11–12	123	652	775
College:			
1–2	20	135	155
3–4	13	49	62
Total	618	1,792	2,410
Median	9.30	10.70	10.26

INTERESTS AND ACTIVITIES IN SCHOOL

Curriculums pursued by graduates and nongraduates.—The percentage of persons reported in this study, who pursued academic curriculums is higher in the Southern regions than in either the Northern or Western region. Data are shown in table 66. Data on curriculums pursued by size of community are given in table VII in appendix A.

Vocational training in high school.—The number and percentage of graduates and nongraduates who had vocational training in high school related to their present jobs are shown in table 67. The percentage was highest, for male nongraduates, in the North Atlantic States and lowest in the South Atlantic; among male graduates it was higher in the Southwestern States and lowest in North Central States. Among female nongraduates the percentage was highest in the North Atlantic States and lowest in the South Atlantic States: among the female graduates it was highest in the Southwestern States and lowest in the South Atlantic.

Value of vocational training in securing work.—Respondents were asked to state whether vocational courses were of assistance in securing work. Tabulations are according to the size of community. In general, a higher percentage of persons in smaller communities than in larger ones indicated that vocational courses helped in securing work. This is true for all groups studied, males and females, and graduates and nongraduates. The percentages indicating that vocational courses assisted in securing work according to size of communities follow:

Size of community	Graduates		Nongraduates	
	Male	Female	Male	Female
1	2	3	4	5
Fewer than 2,500	50.0	65.8	31.8	46.5
2,500 to 24,999	24.7	54.6	11.3	38.3
25,000 to 99,999	17.8	46.2	9.8	22.0
100,000 to 499,999	22.6	41.1	18.7	34.6
500,000 and more	23.6	46.7	17.6	30.2

TABLE 66.—*Number and percent of graduates and nongraduates who pursued given curriculums while in high school, by region*

Curriculum pursued	South Atlantic				South Central				Southwest			
	Graduates		Nongraduates		Graduates		Nongraduates		Graduates		Nongraduates	
	Number	Percent	Number	Percent	Number	Percent	Number	Percent	Number	Percent	Number	Percent
	2	3	4	5	6	7	8	9	10	11	12	18
MALES												
Academic	735	64.0	864	59.6	507	77.2	549	77.5	690	81.3	377	71.0
Trades	221	19.2	331	22.8	30	4.5	21	2.9	14	1.6	27	5.0
Industrial arts	60	5.2	75	5.1	20	3.0	17	2.4	38	4.4	43	8.1
Teacher-training	8	.7	5	.3	14	2.1	4	.5	26	3.6	3	.5
Agriculture	19	1.6	18	1.2	15	2.2	47	6.6	10	1.1	9	1.7
Home economics	3	.2	3	.2	4	.6	2	.2	2	.2	3	.5
Commercial	28	2.4	48	3.3	8	1.2	1	.1	2	.2	4	.7
Other	61	5.3	84	5.8	57	8.6	64	9.0	63	7.4	61	11.4
No response	12	1.0	20	1.3	1	.1	3	.4	3	.3	4	.7
Total	1,147		1,448		656		708		848		531	

Curriculum pursued	North Central				North Atlantic				West			
	Graduates		Nongraduates		Graduates		Nongraduates		Graduates		Nongraduates	
	Number	Percent	Number	Percent	Number	Percent	Number	Percent	Number	Percent	Number	Percent
	14	15	16	17	18	19	20	21	22	23	24	25
Academic	387	59.8	235	41.9	151	65.3	72	34.4	197	50.6	60	32.2
Trades	66	10.2	72	12.8	21	9.0	52	24.8	51	13.1	17	9.1
Industrial arts	25	3.8	58	10.3	19	8.2	28	13.4	46	11.8	52	27.9
Teacher-training	13	2.0	4	.7	4	1.7	1	.4	13	3.3	3	1.6
Agriculture	---		3	.5	---		---		---		---	
Home economics	3	.4	7	1.2	---		---		3	.7	1	.5
Commercial	34	5.2	43	7.6	19	8.2	27	12.9	22	5.6	4	2.1
Other	114	17.6	132	23.5	16	6.9	23	11.0	51	13.1	10	5.3
No response	5	.7	6	1.0	1	.4	4	1.9	4	1.0	39	20.9
Total	647		560		231		209		389		186	

FEMALES

Curriculum pursued	South Atlantic Graduates		South Atlantic Nongraduates		South Central Graduates		South Central Nongraduates		Southwest Graduates		Southwest Nongraduates	
	Number	Percent	Number	Percent	Number	Percent	Number	Percent	Number	Percent	Number	Percent
1	2	3	4	5	6	7	8	9	10	11	12	13
Academic	1,339	67.0	1,241	67.0	902	68.4	854	71.8	1,365	77.3	573	61.2
Trades	67	3.3	115	6.2	4	.3	1	.1	1	.1	4	.4
Industrial arts	58	2.9	83	4.4	7	.5	6	.5	8	.4	15	1.6
Teacher-training	39	2.0	26	1.4	80	6.0	23	1.9	125	7.0	41	4.3
Agriculture	2	.1	4	.2	2		3		1			
Home economics	250	12.5	170	9.1	235	17.8	209	17.5	141	7.9	216	23.0
Commercial	110	5.5	86	4.6	22	1.6	6		8	.4	3	.3
Other	116	5.8	110	5.9	62	4.7	78	6.5	113	6.4	79	8.4
No response	15	.7	16	.8	4	.3	8	.6	2	.1	5	.5
Total	1,996		1,851		1,318		1,188		1,764		936	

Curriculum pursued	North Central Graduates		North Central Nongraduates		North Atlantic Graduates		North Atlantic Nongraduates		West Graduates		West Nongraduates	
	Number	Percent	Number	Percent	Number	Percent	Number	Percent	Number	Percent	Number	Percent
1	14	15	16	17	18	19	20	21	22	23	24	25
Academic	574	49.3	241	32.7	239	52.4	95	31.2	306	47.0	102	30.1
Trades	10	.9	15	2.0	40	8.7	28	9.2	6	.9	3	.8
Industrial arts	15	1.2	12	1.9	17	3.7	19	6.2	8	1.2	10	2.9
Teacher-training	35	3.1	7		15	3.2	11	3.6	26	4.0	7	2.0
Agriculture									1	.1		
Home economics	118	10.1	144	19.5	32	7.0	32	10.5	128	19.6	94	27.8
Commercial	240	20.6	181	24.6	81	17.7	63	20.7	115	17.6	62	18.3
Other	163	14.0	129	17.8	30	6.5	53	17.4	57	8.7	58	17.5
No response	9	.7	6	.8	2	.4	3	.9	3	.4	2	
Total	1,164		735		456		304		650		338	

TABLE 67.—*Number and percent of nongraduates and graduates of high school who had vocational training related to their present job, grade on leaving school, and by region in which school was located*

Region	Grade on leaving school															Graduates	
	Seventh		Eighth		Ninth		Tenth		Eleventh		Twelfth		Total				
	Number	Percent	Number	Percent	Number	Percent	Number	Percent	Number	Percent	Number	Percent	Number	Percent	Number	Percent
1	2	3	4	5	6	7	8	9	10	11	12	13	14	15	16	17
MALES																
South Atlantic	8	33.3	25	8.7	38	12.0	39	13.4	29	15.5	17	24.6	156	13.2	205	21.8
South Central	--	--	--	--	29	12.7	33	16.1	17	17.3	7	25.0	86	14.9	126	22.1
Southwest	2	100.0	13	10.4	16	12.1	21	18.1	16	26.6	2	25.0	70	15.8	180	40.7
North Central	--	--	--	--	12	16.2	25	17.3	23	18.5	12	20.0	72	17.8	91	18.2
North Atlantic	1	25.0	1	50.0	14	35.9	11	24.4	14	27.4	4	21.0	45	28.1	58	30.8
West	--	--	1	100.0	3	7.0	9	18.0	9	26.4	2	9.5	24	15.7	101	29.5
FEMALES																
South Atlantic	5	38.4	33	13.3	93	26.4	78	27.2	53	28.8	26	43.3	288	25.0	483	37.6
South Central	--	--	10	47.6	56	23.7	70	35.1	48	40.0	13	35.1	197	32.2	467	54.6
Southwest	1	50.0	47	34.0	66	46.4	80	52.2	32	40.5	4	66.6	230	44.1	659	56.3
North Central	1	100.0	1	33.3	12	24.4	25	26.3	27	34.6	16	47.0	82	31.5	258	43.8
North Atlantic	--	--	--	--	19	55.8	24	46.1	27	52.9	12	52.1	82	51.2	134	48.7
West	1	50.0	--	--	6	26.0	31	55.3	16	33.3	8	61.5	62	43.6	218	56.6

Employment during high-school attendance.—According to data collected but not shown here, a larger proportion of male graduates than of nongraduates was employed during high-school years, the respective percentages are 55.7 and 44.1. The corresponding percentages for female graduates and non-graduates are 24.5 and 22. The percentages for the different regions follow: For male graduates—South Atlantic, 52; South Central, 63; Southwest, 49; North Atlantic, 52; North Central, 58; and Western, 65. For male non-graduates the percentages are: South Atlantic, 42; South Central, 48; Southwest, 42; North Atlantic, 47; North Central, 44; and Western, 50. The percentages of female graduates employed during their high-school years range from 20 in the South Atlantic region to 34 in the Western. The corresponding range for female nongraduates is from 19.2 in the South Central region to 34 in the North Atlantic. The number of graduates and nongraduates employed during their high-school years according to size of communities in which schools were located is shown in table VIII, of Appendix A.

ACTIVITIES AND INTERESTS AFTER LEAVING SCHOOL

Reasons for leaving day school.—More boys leave high school because of financial needs of the family than for any other reason, according to replies from 3,617 given in table 68. "Desire to make money," and "lack of interest in school," appear to be second and third in importance. The percentages giving these reasons, respectively, are: 28.9, 26.3, and 12.6. The reasons for leaving school most often given by girls, with the percentages are: "Financial needs of family," 22.1; "other," 20.3; "lack of interest," 14.6. "Needed at home," and "desire to make money" rank fourth and fifth; respective percentages are 14.4 and 11.5. Except in a few instances, differences among the geographic regions in reasons for leaving school are slight. A higher percentage of those reporting in the North Central region than in the other regions named "desire to make money," and a lower percentage named "needed at home" as reasons for leaving school. There is close agreement between the North Atlantic and South Atlantic regions in the percentages of persons naming the different reasons for leaving school.

TABLE 68.—*Number and percent¹ of nongraduates indicating reasons for leaving school before graduation, according to geographical region and sex*

Reason for leaving school	Region													
	South Atlantic		South Central		Southwest		North Central		North Atlantic		West		Total	
	Number	Percent	Number	Percent	Number	Percent	Number	Percent	Number	Percent	Number	Percent	Number	Percent
1	2	3	4	5	6	7	8	9	10	11	12	13	14	15
MALE														
Failure in school	62	4.3	31	4.4	24	4.5	13	2.3	10	4.8	22	11.8	162	4.5
Desire to make money	414	28.6	157	22.2	104	19.6	179	32.0	60	28.7	43	23.1	957	26.3
Needed at home	133	9.2	63	8.9	95	17.9	29	5.2	20	9.6	20	10.8	360	9.9
Financial needs of family	428	29.6	212	29.0	137	25.8	173	30.9	57	27.3	45	24.2	1,052	28.9
Did not like teacher	22	1.5	7	1.0	21	4.0	6	1.1	2	1.0	2	1.1	59	1.6
Lack of relation between school and vocation chosen	34	2.4	10	1.4	9	1.7	9	1.6	6	2.9	6	3.2	74	2.0
Poor health	45	3.1	29	4.1	23	4.3	14	2.5	9	4.4	2	1.1	122	3.4
Lack of interest	169	11.7	125	17.7	56	10.6	65	11.6	23	11.0	20	10.8	458	12.6
Other	133	9.2	70	9.9	60	11.3	66	11.7	19	9.1	25	13.4	373	10.2
Total	1,439	--------	704	--------	529	--------	554	--------	206	--------	185	--------	3,617	--------
FEMALE														
Failure in school	100	5.4	35	2.9	45	4.8	14	1.9	13	4.3	22	6.5	229	4.3
Desire to make money	258	13.9	91	7.7	76	8.1	76	10.3	63	20.7	51	15.1	615	11.5
Needed at home	299	16.2	144	12.1	163	17.4	103	14.0	37	12.2	23	6.8	769	14.4
Financial needs of family	423	22.9	293	24.7	190	20.3	149	20.3	66	21.7	61	18.1	1,182	22.1
Did not like teacher	22	1.2	14	1.2	25	2.7	10	1.4	3	1.0	2	.6	76	1.4
Lack of relation between school and vocation chosen	37	2.0	10	.8	11	1.2	13	1.8	4	1.3	2	.6	77	1.4
Poor health	171	9.2	106	8.9	72	7.7	67	9.1	28	9.2	37	11.0	481	9.0
Lack of interest	247	13.3	213	17.9	132	14.1	102	13.9	33	10.9	46	13.6	773	14.6
Other	272	14.7	274	23.0	216	23.0	186	25.4	46	15.1	92	27.3	1,086	20.3
Total	1,829	--------	1,180	--------	930	--------	720	--------	293	--------	336	--------	5,288	--------

¹ Computed on total number of cases, including 25 "no response," from males and 64 "no response" from females.

Reasons for attending evening school.—The chief reason given by students for attending evening school is to "prepare for new type of work" (table 69). For the group as a whole (1,991 cases), the main reasons given for attending evening school with the percentage of students are: "To prepare for new type of work", 35.5; and "to improve chances for an increase in rank or salary," 22. The third ranking reason is "to gain general information for social and cultural background," 16.2 percent.

Activities followed immediately after leaving high school.—The period between formal schooling and entrance into occupational activity is an important one. Data were collected from persons enrolled in evening school concerning the activities followed immediately after leaving day school (table 70). A larger percentage of males in the Southern region went directly to work than in the Northern region, and a smaller percentage "sought work without success." A similar difference existed among the females. Data now shown here indicate that 241, or 6.9 percent, of the male high-school graduates have never been employed; and 279, or 8.3 percent, of the nongraduates. Of the female graduates 1,460, or 21.7 percent, were never employed, and 1,422, or 28.5 percent, of the female nongraduates. Data show slight differences among the communities of different sizes in the number of jobs held by graduates and nongraduates after leaving school. For all communities combined the medians are, respectively: Male graduates and nongraduates, 1.92 and 1.89; female graduates and nongraduates, 1.67 and 1.58.

TABLE 69.—*Reasons for attending evening school, by region (1,991 cases)*

Reason for attending school	Male	Female	Total	Percent
1	2	3	4	5
To keep up with developments in present job	79	196	275	13. 8
To prepare for new type of work	168	539	707	35. 5
To gain general information for social and cultural background	100	222	322	16. 2
To improve chances for an increase in rank or salary	148	290	438	22. 0
To get courses which cannot be taken in day school	36	96	132	6. 6
To get credits for graduation from high school	50	175	225	11. 3
To get credit for entrance to college	66	101	167	8. 4
To prepare for civil service examinations	40	93	133	6. 7
Other reasons	25	77	102	5. 1

TABLE 70.—*Activity followed by evening school students after leaving day school according to grade-level attained*

SOUTHERN REGION

Activity	Elementary				High school		College		Total	Per-cent
	1	2–4	5–6	7–8	9–10	11–12	1–2	3–4		
1	2	3	4	5	6	7	8	9	10	11
MALES										
Went directly to work		24	45	62	55	26	6	4	222	78.4
Helped at home	1	2	1	6	4	5			19	6.7
Worked with parents at home		2	3	6	1	2	1		15	5.3
Traveled			1	1	2	3			7	2.5
Took vacation (over 3 months)				3	2				5	1.8
Sought employment without success				2	4	2	2		10	3.5
Other				2	1	1		1	5	1.8
Total	1	28	50	82	69	39	9	5	283	100.0
FEMALES										
Went directly to work		17	59	124	92	87	7	1	387	48.9
Helped at home		3	15	36	35	45	3		137	17.3
Became housewife		3	9	25	34	42	2	2	117	14.8
Worked with parents at home		2	4	16	14	15			51	6.4
Traveled			1	4	3	3	1		12	1.5
Took vacation (over 3 months)			1	3	3	13			20	2.5
Sought employment without success		1		5	6	21	3		36	4.5
Other		1	1	3	13	10	3	1	32	4.1
Total		27	90	216	200	236	19	4	792	100.0
TOTAL										
Went directly to work		41	104	186	147	113	13	5	609	56.7
Helped at home	1	5	16	42	39	50	3		156	14.5
Became housewife		3	9	25	34	42	2	2	117	10.9
Worked with parents at home		4	7	22	15	17	1		66	6.1
Traveled			2	5	5	6	1		19	1.8
Took vacation (over 3 months)			1	6	5	13			25	2.3
Sought employment without success		1		7	10	23	5		46	4.3
Other		1	1	5	14	11	3	2	37	3.4
Total	1	55	140	298	269	275	28	9	1,075	100.0

NORTHERN REGION

Activity	Elementary				High school		College		Total	Per-cent
MALES										
Went directly to work	2	5	10	61	64	30	2		174	70.5
Helped at home	1	2				3			6	2.4
Worked with parents at home		1	1	3	2	1			8	3.2
Traveled		1		3	3	5			12	4.9
Took vacation (more than 3 months)				1		2			3	1.2
Sought employment without success				3	22	9			34	13.8
Other			2	2	3	3			10	4.0
Total	3	9	13	73	94	53	2		247	100.0

TABLE 70.—*Activity followed by evening school students after leaving day school, according to grade-level attained*—Continued

NORTHERN REGION—Continued

Activity	Elementary				High school		College		Other	Total	Percent
	1	2–4	5–6	7–8	9–10	11–12	1–2	3–4			
FEMALES											
Went directly to work	------	4	8	60	81	109	20	------	------	282	46.2
Helped at home	------	2	5	19	23	36	4	------	------	89	14.6
Became housewife	------	2	7	19	19	18	2	------	------	67	10.9
Worked with parents at home	------	3	2	6	2	15	1	------	------	29	4.8
Traveled	------	------	------	------	3	2	5	------	1	------	11	1.8
Took vacation (more than 3 months)	------	------	------	5	5	6	1	------	------	17	2.8
Sought employment without success	------	------	------	8	17	35	2	------	------	62	10.2
Other	------	1	3	------	19	26	------	3	1	53	8.7
Total	------	12	25	120	168	250	30	4	1	610	100.0
TOTAL											
Went directly to work	2	9	18	121	145	139	22	------	------	456	53.2
Helped at home	1	4	5	19	23	39	4	------	------	95	11.1
Became housewife	------	2	7	19	19	18	2	------	------	67	7.8
Worked with parents at home	------	4	3	9	4	16	1	------	------	37	4.3
Traveled	------	1	------	6	5	10	------	1	------	23	2.7
Took vacation (more than 3 months)	------	------	------	6	5	8	1	------	------	20	2.3
Sought employment without success	------	------	------	11	39	44	2	------	------	96	11.2
Other	------	1	5	2	22	29	------	3	1	63	7.4
Total	3	21	38	193	262	303	32	4	1	857	100.0

Means of obtaining job.—The number and percent of graduates and non-graduates and the methods used to secure jobs are shown in table 71. In the main, the highest percentage obtained their jobs through friends; the next, by direct application; and the next through relatives. A small proportion received assistance from the school. In order to obtain direct information along this line, respondents were asked if the "school authorities rendered aid in obtaining employment." The number and percentage replying in the affirmative were: Male graduates, 335, or 8.8 percent; male nongraduates, 119, or 3.4 percent; female graduates, 636, or 9.3 percent; and female nongraduates, 142, or 3 percent.

The educational levels reached by evening school students and the methods used to obtain their first job are shown in table 72. Those receiving aid from teachers or the placement bureau of the school had attended school longer than other groups; the median years are 11.89 for the Northern and 11.64 for the Southern students. This is probably because high schools have employment agencies. It is also in line with the general policy of the schools to aid those who have better training. Those who obtained their first job through the assistance of former students had attended school the least; the medians are 8.67 years for the Northern students, and 8.60 for the Southern students.   In all these data, it will be noted that the highest percentage of students obtained their jobs through friends.   The method named by the next highest percentage is "personal search" or "direct application."

Wages in first job.—The number and median years of schooling and the wages received per week on their first job are given in table 73.   Among males, there is a definite increase in wages as the education increases until the second-year high-school level is reached.

TABLE 71.—*Number and percent of high-school graduates and nongraduates and methods used to secure their present jobs*

Means of securing present job	Male				Female			
	Graduates		Nongraduates		Graduates		Nongraduates	
	Number	Percent	Number	Percent	Number	Percent	Number	Percent
1	2	3	4	5	6	7	8	9
Public employment agency	180	4.6	244	6.7	317	4.5	212	4.1
Private employment agency	57	1.5	60	1.6	86	1.2	87	1.7
Relatives	578	14.9	553	15.2	764	10.8	660	12.7
Friends	1,141	29.4	1,030	28.3	1,752	24.6	1,176	22.6
Public-school placement bureau	13	.3	13	.4	52	.7	15	.3
Principal or teacher	94	2.4	26	.7	174	2.4	21	.4
Direct application	1,168	30.0	964	26.5	1,307	18.4	639	12.3
Own business	40	1.0	18	.5	30	.4	19	.4
Total	3,271		2,908		4,482		2,829	
No job at present	617	15.9	729	20.1	2,626	37.0	2,361	45.5

TABLE 72.—*Means used by evening school students in securing their first jobs, according to median years in school*

Means of securing first job	Region			
	Southern		Northern and western	
	Number	Median years in school	Number	Median years in school
1	2	3	4	5
Persons worked for before graduation	50	10.14	65	9.64
Personal search for job	233	9.73	204	10.67
Advertisement by self in paper	32	9.55	23	11.19
Public employment agency	57	8.86	42	10.69
Business connection of family	72	9.26	75	10.35
Personal friends	434	8.97	300	10.09
Former students of school	16	8.60	12	8.67
Teacher or placement bureau of high school	23	11.64	24	11.89
Private employment agency	12	10.33	29	10.63
Other	48	11.10	49	11.25
Total	977	9.47	823	10.75

Relationship of sons' to fathers' occupation.—Do Negro sons tend to follow their fathers' occupation?   In an attempt to answer this question, inquiry was made concerning the jobs which were held longest by graduates and nongraduates. The jobs which were held longest were compared with the fathers' occupations in order to discount the transitory nature of many jobs held during the depression. According to the data in table 74, 17.2 percent of the male graduates and 22 percent of the male nongraduates were following their fathers' occupations. In a follow-up study of 1,600 high-school pupils on the Pacific Coast, Proctor [1] found that 13 percent of the sons were found in the same occupations as their fathers. When "rank of occupation [2] is used as the basis of comparison regarding occupational status, it is found that the picture changes materially," reported Proctor. "In this situation, it was discovered that 51 percent of the sons were in occupations having the same rank as that of their fathers." In interpreting the data in this survey regarding relationship of sons' and fathers' occupations, the general social and economic status of the group should be remembered. In view of this status, a lower correlation is to be expected among them than among the white group whose general social and economic culture is in advance of that of Negroes. As Negroes' educational level increases, under normal circumstances, their occupational status should improve. The fact that the occupations of the Negro male nongraduates in this study had a closer relationship to their fathers' occupation than the male graduates seems to substantiate this generalization.

TABLE 73.—*Median years of schooling of evening-school students and wages per week in first job*

Wages per week	Region			
	Northern and western		Southern	
	Number	Median	Number	Median
1	2	3	4	5
	MALE			
$5 or less	33	9.88	73	7.63
$6 to $10	79	9.65	73	8.52
$11 to $15	70	10.44	56	9.74
$16 to $20	37	9.93	26	9.57
$21 to $25	22	9.89	18	
$26 or more	6		4	
Total	247	9.85	250	7.51
	FEMALE			
$5 or less	104	9.50	292	8.84
$6 to $10	199	11.91	275	9.86
$11 to $15	132	11.32	80	11.23
$16 to $20	35	12.00	12	
$21 to $25	15		10	
$26 or more	8		8	
Total	493	11.21	677	9.69

[1] Proctor, William M. A thirteen year follow-up of high school pupils' occupations. The vocational guidance magazine, 15: 306–10, January 1937.

[2] According to the Barr scale.

TABLE 74.—*Relation between occupations which were held longest and father's occupation*

Occupation in which employed longest	Not employed	Father's occupation													No response	Total
		Agriculture	Forestry and fishing	Extraction of minerals	Manufacturing and mechanical industries	Transportation and communication	Trade	Public service	Professional service	Semiprofessional service	Domestic and personal service	Clerical occupations	Other		
	2	3	4	5	6	7	8	9	10	11	12	13	14	15	16
								GRADUATES								
Agriculture: Number	8	37		1	3		3		3		1		7	7	70
Percent		15.29			0.69		2.48		2.13		0.22		0.75		1.84
Forestry and fishing: Number															
Percent															
Extraction of minerals: Number	1										1		4		6
Percent											0.22		0.43		0.16
Manufacturing and mechanical industries: Number	43	23			75	18	6	20			24		81	76	366
Percent		9.50			17.16	12.41	4.96	18.52			5.23		8.66		9.62
Transportation and communication: Number	19	8			11	11	12	7	4		16	1	40	23	141
Percent		3.31			2.52	7.59	9.92	6.48	2.84		3.49	4.55	4.28		3.70
Trade: Number	35	13		2	40	11	24	8	13	1	39	2	91	98	377
Percent		5.37			9.15	7.59	19.83	7.41	9.22		8.50	9.09	9.73		9.91
Public service: Number	4	2		1	2	1	2	3	3		5	1	6	10	40
Percent		0.83			0.46	0.69	1.65	2.78	2.13		1.09	4.55	0.64		1.05
Professional service: Number	24	36		2	21	8	7	7	24	1	32	4	44	74	284
Percent		14.88			4.81	5.52	5.79	6.48	17.02		6.97	18.18	4.71		7.46
Semiprofessional service: Number	2				3			1		1	4		1	4	16
Percent					0.69			0.98			0.87		0.11		0.42
Domestic and personal service: Number	132	75	2	5	161	62	28	32	59	1	216	10	330	251	1,364
Percent		30.99			36.84	42.76	23.14	29.63	41.84		47.06	45.45	35.29		35.84
Clerical occupations: Number	11	3			12	1	10	8	2	1	10	2	26	45	131
Percent		1.24			2.75	0.69	8.26	7.41	1.42		2.18	9.09	2.78		3.44

	C1	C2	C3	C4	C5	C6	C7	C8	C9	C10	C11	C12	C13	C14	C15
Other: Number / Percent	111	44 / 18.18	1	3	109 / 24.94	44 / 30.34	29 / 23.97	21 / 19.44	32 / 22.70	3	111 / 24.18	2 / 9.09	299 / 31.98	191	1,000 / 26.27
Total[1]	391	242	3	14	437	145	121	108	141	8	459	22	935	780	3,806
NONGRADUATES															
Agriculture: Number / Percent	13	79 / 31.85	1		2 / 0.56		1 / 1.67		3 / 3.30	1			5 / 0.54	20	124 / 3.51
Forestry and fishing: Number / Percent					1 / 0.28							5			10 / 0.28
Extraction of minerals: Number / Percent	2														
Manufacturing and mechanical industries: Number / Percent	46	20 / 8.06		1 / 7.14	92 / 25.77	11 / 9.02	3 / 5.00	1 / 1.41	7 / 7.69		21 / 6.27	1	89 / 9.62	85	378 / 10.69
Transportation and communication: Number / Percent	19	14 / 5.65			13 / 3.64	10 / 8.20	4 / 6.67	5 / 7.04	4 / 4.40		18 / 5.37	2	56 / 6.05	39	184 / 5.20
Trade: Number / Percent	30	11 / 4.44		1 / 7.14	38 / 10.64	14 / 11.48	15 / 25.00	9 / 12.68	3 / 3.30		26 / 7.76	2	59 / 6.38	77	285 / 8.06
Public service: Number / Percent	1	2 / 0.81			2 / 0.56			1 / 1.41	2 / 2.20		4 / 1.19		4 / 0.43	4	20 / 0.57
Professional service: Number / Percent	10	4 / 1.61			3 / 0.84	5 / 4.10	2 / 3.33	4 / 5.63	9 / 9.90		7 / 2.09		16 / 1.73	20	80 / 2.26
Semiprofessional service: Number / Percent	2										1 / 0.30		1 / 0.11	5	9 / 0.25
Domestic and personal service: Number / Percent	133	64 / 25.81	1	6 / 42.86	105 / 29.41	37 / 30.33	12 / 20.00	25 / 35.21	40 / 43.96	1	156 / 46.57	7	286 / 30.92	276	1,148 / 32.47
Clerical occupations: Number / Percent	6	1 / 0.40		1 / 7.14	6 / 1.68	2 / 1.64	4 / 6.67	5 / 7.04	2 / 2.20		6 / 1.79		12 / 1.30	19	64 / 1.81
Other: Number / Percent	136	53 / 21.37		5 / 35.71	94 / 26.33	43 / 35.25	18 / 30.00	21 / 29.58	20 / 21.98	1	96 / 28.66	5	392 / 42.38	340	1,225 / 34.64
Total[2]	398	248	2	14	357	122	60	71	91	3	335	14	925	888	3,536

[1] 11 persons not employed included in total.

[2] 9 persons not employed included in total.

NOTE.—Read table thus: Of the 242 persons whose fathers are engaged in agriculture, 37, or 15.29 percent, have held jobs in the agricultural field longer than in any other of the 437 whose fathers are engaged in manufacturing and mechanical industries, 75, or 17.16 percent, also held jobs longest in these occupations; 11, or 2.52 percent, held jobs longest in the transportation and communications field, and 161, or 36.84 percent, worked in domestic and personal service longest.

TABLE 75.—*Percent¹ of graduates and nongraduates working for designated employer, according to region and sex (13,496 cases)*

Region	Working for—															
	Negro concern				Self				White concern				Government			
	Male		Female		Male		Female		Male		Female		Male		Female	
	Graduates	Nongraduates	Graduates	Nongraduates	Graduates	Nongraduates	Graduates	Nongraduates	Graduates	Nongraduates	Graduates	Nongraduates	Graduates	Nongraduates	Graduates	Nongraduates
1	2	3	4	5	6	7	8	9	10	11	12	13	14	15	16	17
South Atlantic	14.9	10.9	14.7	7.0	5.2	4.0	4.2	2.6	65.3	74.2	60.4	81.1	11.2	8.4	15.6	4.5
South Central	13.3	9.9	12.9	9.7	6.4	7.1	3.0	4.8	64.7	70.8	63.1	73.5	10.9	5.4	17.2	6.4
Southwest	12.5	13.5	12.1	7.7	6.7	3.3	3.6	6.1	68.0	73.3	64.2	77.3	8.9	6.5	13.9	5.2
North Central	11.5	8.7	18.6	13.5	3.3	1.9	2.3	3.3	65.4	69.0	54.1	67.4	17.5	18.0	18.2	13.1
North Atlantic	16.9	7.6	19.1	9.3	1.5	1.9	3.3	1.2	64.0	67.5	53.6	76.4	15.8	20.3	20.2	10.5
Western	12.5	5.0	15.7	8.0	2.4	4.2	3.7	2.2	73.0	75.0	65.8	72.0	11.6	12.8	12.4	13.2

¹ Percentages for other employers not included here.

Employers.—Inquiry was made concerning the employers of graduates, nongraduates, and evening-school students. Replies are shown in tables 75 and 76. The percent of male graduates employed by Negroes range from 11.5 in the North Central region to 16.9 in the North Atlantic region (table 75). Fewer nongraduates find employment in Negro concerns than graduates, the percent ranging from 7.6 in the North Atlantic region to 13.5 in the Southwest. The proportion of male graduates employed by the local State, or Federal Government is greater than that of the nongraduates in the Southern regions, but less in the Northern and Western regions. Further details may be observed from the table. Of the total number of graduates and nongraduates studied, 7,139, or slightly more than a third, were not employed at the time of the investigation. A smaller proportion of the male evening-school students in the South and a larger proportion in the North and West worked for Negro concerns than among the high-school graduates and nongraduates. This is also true of the females. Information concerned with evening-school students is given in table 76.

Relation of present job to first job.—Table 77 shows the number of evening-school students employed in a given occupation according to their first job. The largest percent of persons who have not changed their type of occupations was in domestic and personal service, especially among women.

TABLE 76.—*Percent* [1] *of evening-school students indicating their present employer, by region* (*929 cases*)

Region	Employed by—							
	Negro concern		Self		White concern		Government	
	Male	Female	Male	Female	Male	Female	Male	Female
1	2	3	4	5	6	7	8	9
Southern_____	5.4	5.7	5.9	12.7	57.1	66.0	23.2	4.5
Northern and western_____	16.2	24.5	7.4	7.1	62.5	48.1	12.5	9.5

[1] Percentages for other employers not included here.

TABLE 77.—*Number of evening-school students, present jobs, and first jobs*

Present job	Agriculture		Manufacturing and mechanical industries		Transportation		Trade and industry		Professional service		Domestic and personal service		Other		Clerical		Total	
	Male	Female	Male	Female	Male	Female	Male	Female	Male	Female	Male	Female	Male	Female	Male	Female	Male	Female
1	**2**	**3**	**4**	**5**	**6**	**7**	**8**	**9**	**10**	**11**	**12**	**13**	**14**	**15**	**16**	**17**	**18**	**19**
Agriculture	8	2	2	1	1				1		6						18	3
Manufacturing and mechanical industries	1		8	21	2		1	2			6	11					18	37
Transportation and communication					3		1				2						6	
Trade				6	1		6	9			3	7					10	19
Professional service		1	4	9			1	7	3	20	1	9	2			5	6	41
Domestic and personal service	2		1		1		1	1	1	11	34	170	2		1	7	45	205
Clerical			3		1		1	1	1		2	10	1		1	24	6	36
Other					1		1		1		6		1		1		14	
Total	11	3	18	37	9		11	20	7	36	60	207	5		2	38	123	341

READ TABLE VERTICALLY THUS: Of the 11 males whose first jobs were in agriculture, 8 are now engaged in agriculture, 1 in manufacturing and mechanical industries, and 2 in domestic and personal service. Of the 36 females whose first jobs were in the professions, 20 are now engaged in the professions, 11 in domestic and personal service, and 2 in trades, etc.

CHAPTER X

Vocational Guidance in Secondary Schools and Colleges for Negroes

ORGANIZATION AND ADMINISTRATION OF GUIDANCE

INFORMATION concerned with provisions for guidance was obtained from 159 high schools and 44 colleges for Negroes. Four of the 11 organization plans for guidance reported by these institutions are outlined briefly in this paragraph. Guidance functions are entrusted to a committee of interested teachers in 68 high schools and 13 colleges. Sixteen high schools and two colleges use a central bureau of vocational guidance, with a director and trained staff responsible to the superintendent, for the entire school system in which each was located. Thirteen high schools and three colleges maintain a central guidance bureau within their institutions. Eleven high schools and two colleges employed trained vocational counselors. Fifty-two percent of the high schools and 45 percent of the colleges had no definite guidance organization.

Officers performing guidance functions.—Twenty different officers and teachers perform guidance functions in the 138 high schools and 18 officers and teachers in the 35 colleges reporting. In the high schools the principal is most frequently in charge of guidance; among the colleges, the dean. In the high schools the homeroom teacher is next; in the colleges, the registrar. Others in high schools in charge of guidance are: Vocational teacher, teacher of civics, counselor, class adviser, and assistant principal. In the colleges, the dean of men, the dean of women, and guidance committees assume the functions. The following is a list of other officers with the number of institutions reporting each: Dean of girls, 8; playground instructor, 5; registrar, 4; health worker, 3; Smith-Hughes worker, 3; dean of boys, 3; psychiatric worker, Jeanes worker, and secretary to the president, 1 each. The number of different officers responsible for guidance is indicative of its uncertain status as a function of schools and colleges for Negroes.

Proportion of teachers having a part in guidance.—While it is desirable that the major functions of guidance should be conducted by certain definite officers, all teachers should participate. At least, they should have close enough contact with it to understand its purposes and to see and apply its implications. Data collected in this study show that a large proportion of the

111

teachers participate in the guidance programs. A majority of the teachers assist in guidance in 60 high schools and 6 colleges; about half in 24 high schools and 7 colleges; and a third in 43 high schools and 16 colleges.

Officers having general charge of guidance.—In table 78 information is given concerning the officers who have general charge of guidance. As with officers performing guidance functions, there is little agreement in practice. Again, the principal is most frequently in charge in the high schools; in the colleges, the dean.

GUIDANCE FUNCTIONS AND SERVICES

Type of functions.—Eight different guidance functions were performed by officers and teachers in the colleges and high schools replying. Counseling is carried on in 66 colleges and 121 high schools. Other functions, with the number of institutions in which each operates, are: (1) Instruction in occupational information—colleges, 12; high schools, 90. (2) Placement—colleges, 21; high schools, 28. (3) Advise with parents—colleges, 33; high schools, 4. (4) Recording and using data—colleges, 12; high schools, 26. (5) Make occupational studies and prepare guidance material—colleges, 6; high schools, 13. (6) Make follow-up studies—colleges, 7; high schools, 10. (7) Testing—colleges, 6; high schools, 19.

Services available.—One hundred and six high schools and 23 colleges responded to the inquiry concerning guidance activities and services. Approximately one-half the high schools and nearly two-thirds of the colleges provide some guidance for first-year students. The percentage of high schools and colleges offering guidance to all students is 41 and 57, respectively. The number of high schools offering guidance according to the groups is: Second-year, 29; third-year, 31; fourth-year, 35; of colleges—sophomores, 4; juniors, 4; seniors, 8. The following is a list of guidance services available in the schools and colleges reporting: Orientation courses, lectures, conferences, general vocational training, placement bureau, psychological and psychiatric services, recreational guidance, health service, courses in citizenship, social guidance, and follow-up services.

TABLE 78.—*Officers in charge of guidance*

Officer	Number of institutions reporting		Officer	Number of institutions reporting	
	High schools	Colleges		High schools	Colleges
1	2	3	1	2	3
Principal	87	6	Class adviser	2	
Counselor	7	2	Group adviser	1	
Superintendent	3		Guidance committee	6	4
Vocational teacher	6	2	Teacher of civics, economics, etc.	5	
Dean of boys	2		Dean of men		1
Dean of women	1	1	Dean of college		12
Homeroom teacher	2	1	Personnel director		3
Vice principal	3		Registrar, clerk		1

COLLECTION AND USE OF INFORMATION

Information about students.—Procedures used in obtaining information about students in high schools and colleges are shown in table 79. "Conferences" head the list, followed by "tests" in high schools and by "school records" in colleges. The institutions consider "information about family status" as the most important kind of information for guidance purposes according to replies, as shown in table 80. "Scholarship record" is next in importance for both groups of institutions, followed by "physical condition of student," and "vocational preferences" in the colleges. Further details may be observed in the table. The procedures used for this purpose with the number of institutions reporting each are shown in table 81. According to these data, "exploratory courses" and "autobiographies" are the most frequently used procedures in assisting students to obtain information about themselves. It is conceivable that in some cases information which is obtained is not put to practical use. It is therefore of interest to note the ways in which the institutions in this study used the information. This is shown in table 82.

TABLE 79.—*Sources and procedures used in obtaining information about students*

Procedure	Number of institutions reporting		Procedure	Number of institutions reporting	
	High schools	Colleges		High schools	Colleges
1	2	3	1	2	3
Conferences	115	28	Personal history	6	6
Tests	49	11	Medical examination	6	4
Aptitude tests	16	13	Observation of pupil by teacher	6	
School records	41	9	Personality rating	1	4
Home visitations	16		Follow-up studies	10	1
Classroom discussions	2		References	1	1
School organizations	3		Correspondence with parents		1
General information blanks	6	7	Assemblies	2	
Placement tests	2	9	Field trips	2	
Psychological tests	1	5			

Information about occupations.—Information usually sought by institutions about occupations includes such items as education, health, and physical requirements of candidates for jobs; supply and demand of workers; working conditions; remuneration and other compensations; and general status of the occupation. The procedures used in obtaining occupational information with number of institutions reporting each follow: (1) Followup of graduates and employed students—high school, 63; college, 15. (2) Contacts with employment centers and employers—high school, 38; college, 13. (3) Occupational surveys and research—high school, 34; college, 6. Fifty-six of the high schools and sixteen of the colleges did not respond to this question. Table 83 gives the procedures used by the institutions in assisting students to obtain knowledge of occupations. Recognizing that knowledge gained about occupations is useless unless it is put at the disposal of students and school officers for guidance purposes, the institutions included in this study reported the following ways in which occupational information was used: (1) In interviews and conferences; (2) in bulletins, pamphlets, and scrapbooks; (3) in making up content material for subjects on guidance; (4) in vocational forum discussions; (5) in counseling on occupational decisions; and (6) in the organization of assembly programs.

TABLE 80.—*Kind of information obtained about students*

Kind of information	Number of institutions reporting		Kind of information	Number of institutions reporting	
	High schools	Colleges		High schools	Colleges
1	2	3	1	2	3
Family status	109	32	Achievement and intelligence tests	27	9
Scholarship record	82	28	Vocational preferences	9	11
Physical condition of pupils	46	11	Personal history	10	14
Social records	4	2	Personality ratings	29	8
Pupil's dominant interest	22	7	Recommendations	----	4
Pupil's aptitude	5	2	Extracurricular interests	2	4

TABLE 81.—*Procedures used in assisting students to obtain information about themselves*

Procedure	Number of institutions reporting		Procedure	Number of institutions reporting	
	High schools	Colleges		High schools	Colleges
1	2	3	1	2	3
Questionnaires	3	----	Extracurricular activity	19	4
Exploratory courses	37	7	Tests	5	4
Autobiographies	34	8	Courses in hygiene	3	1
Biographic readings	4	2	Vocational guidance program	4	----
Conferences	26	4	Surveys	4	----
Self-analysis blanks	12	1	Lectures	5	----
Orientation courses	3	6	Time study charts	----	2
Field trips	19	----	Courses in biology	----	1
Assemblies	19	5			

TABLE 82.—*Ways in which information about students is used for guidance purposes*

Information used in—	Number of institutions reporting		Information used in—	Number of institutions reporting	
	High schools	Colleges		High schools	Colleges
1	2	3	1	2	3
Counseling	108	28	School publications	7	2
Lectures on vocational guidance	12	3	Vocational explorations	7	5
Group conferences	13	----	Advice to parents	1	----
Special assignment	3	----	Scholarship guides	----	1
Assembly programs	23	5	Choosing college	3	----
Clubs	1	1			

Special guidance procedures and activities.—Unless a system of accurate and available records is maintained, the time and energy used in securing information about students and occupations are wasted. Among the new devices for recording data is the cumulative record card. This record affords a fairer appraisal of the student than isolated items of information. It was used by one-half of the institutions replying. Permanent record cards of scholastic work were maintained by 53 colleges and 14 high schools. Other kinds of records kept, with the number of institutions keeping them, follow: Folders—college, 9, high school, 1; loose-leaf record sheets—college, 4; graphic records—college, 6, high school, 6; health records—college 7, high school, 1; ledger—college, 2. While several kinds of records are kept by the institutions replying, few made definite use of the data recorded for guidance purposes. Three colleges use the data for ability grouping; five colleges and three high schools for counseling and research purposes; and one high school for remedial work. Officials using records with number of institutions in which each type is used follow: (1) School officials and faculty—college, 50, high school, 16; (2) guidance functionaries—college, 6, high school, 1; (3) prospective employers—college, 3, high school, 1.

TABLE 83.—*Procedures and sources used in informing students about occupations*

Procedure and source	Number of institutions reporting		Procedure and source	Number of institutions reporting	
	High schools	Colleges		High schools	Colleges
1	2	3	1	2	3
Lectures and assembly programs__	101	29	Contacts with industrial, trade, and commercial establishments_	6	-------
The general curriculum_____	16	8	Radio_____	2	2
Conferences, discussions, etc_____	59	21	Movies_____	5	-------
Guidance and occupational courses	26	5	Occupational surveys_____	4	2
Field trips, observation tours, etc_____	38	5	Counseling_____	1	-------
Library assignments, general and vocational literature_____	30	21	No response_____	43	10

Eighty-three high schools and 33 colleges conducted placement and follow-up services. Some of the means by which these services were given with kind and number of institutions using them are: By direct contact with employers—19 high schools, 10 colleges; employment service—40 high schools, 19 colleges; follow-up studies—39 high schools, 13 colleges; alumni organizations—4 high schools, 1 college; correspondence through principal's office—3 high schools and 2 colleges. Placement and follow-up of former students are beginning to be considered as important functions of guidance. The effectiveness of occupational training can only be measured in the occupation; while only a few of the institutions studied conduct placement and follow-up services, they set an example which can be widely followed. Another phase of this subject has to do with the procedures used in relating vocational training to opportunities and conditions of work in the area served by the institution. Fifty-four of the 207 high schools selected for special study stated that no effort was made along this line. The procedures used by 153 high schools and 24 colleges are given in table 84. Among other activities and organizations used for guidance purposes by a few institutions in addition to those mentioned are the following: Home projects, fraternities, guidance week, student advisory committees, forums, and occupational exhibits.

TABLE 84.—*Procedures used to relate vocational training to opportunities and conditions of work*

Procedure	Number of institutions reporting	
	Colleges	High schools
Inform pupils concerning vocational opportunities	19	125
Secure information concerning pupils' abilities, interests, and aptitudes	17	120
Provide organized placement service	13	31
Provide follow-up of students after they enter occupations	17	58
Obtain judgment of employers on the educational needs of students or graduates in their employ	16	72
Appoint permanent advisory committees of parents and patrons	1	32
Appoint permanent guidance committees of teachers	10	62

TABLE 85.—*Guidance objectives with number of institutions establishing each*

Objective	Number of institutions reporting—	
	High schools	Colleges
To guide student in choice of suitable vocation, according to individual aptitude and ability	22	----------
To compile occupational information for students, according to community possibilities	11	5
To aid students in securing knowledge of own strength, limitations, abilities, and aptitudes, and help to formulate goals	8	6
To give recognition to personality variances in individuals, and concentration of training on character and development of personality	7	----------
To teach the importance of efficiency in all lines of endeavor	6	1
To counsel in preparation for higher vocational and educational pursuits according to ability of individual student	6	----------
To develop ability to participate effectively in cultural life of Nation	9	2
To train for good citizenship	6	2
To give guidance in correct methods of studying occupations in order intelligently to choose life work	10	8
To direct interests of pupils toward development of home community	4	1
To show importance of development of sound health	3	----------
To guide in development of a wholesome, happy, and comfortable home life	5	----------
To train for worthy use of leisure time	2	----------
To assist in occupational placement in order to make for economic security	2	2
To study occupational trends	1	2
To prepare for immediate service in simple tasks (maid, janitor, etc.)	1	----------
To give a definite understanding of the occupational problems of Negroes	1	2
To develop interest and pride in own race	1	----------
To educate the head, heart, and hand	1	----------
To teach importance of student's personal satisfaction and enjoyment in work	2	2
To assist in building Christian character	----------	1
To develop proficiency in more than one vocation	----------	1
To show that there is no definite demarcation between vocational and educational guidance	----------	1
To prepare for leadership in professional fields	----------	2
To enable the student to utilize more effectively all the educational opportunities of his collegiate experience both on and off the campus	----------	1

The objectives of the guidance program with the number of institutions naming each are given in table 85. According to the data furnished there is considerable variation among the institutions in the stated objectives. Only 61 high schools and 21 colleges replied to the inquiry concerning objectives. Twenty-two of the high schools reported that the objective of their guidance program was "To guide pupils in the choice of suitable vocations, according to individual aptitude and ability." This objective is stated more than any other by the high schools. The objective stated by the greatest number of colleges was "To aid students in securing knowledge of strength, limitations, abilities, and aptitudes, and to help formulate goals." From the data presented it appears that there is a need for greater clarification and specification of objectives, and a better adjustment between them and the guidance machinery.

CONCLUSIONS

Opportunities available.—Opportunities for guidance service are limited in the institutions replying. Only 602 of 2,578 institutions for Negroes offered such services. Of that number, definite information concerning the guidance program in operation was received from 159 high schools and 44 colleges. Not only are there relatively few institutions providing guidance, but the programs are limited as shown by the number gathering information about students, about occupations, and about the social and economic life of the community, and by the opportunities offered students to gain occupational experience. Moreover, few institutions make use of the information after it is gathered, or relate the educational program to occupational needs.

Characteristics of a good guidance program.—Vocational guidance should be considered as one phase of the general problem of guidance, and both as a part of the total educational process. According to Jones and Hand,[1] one of the major functions of education is to develop in each individual "a fundamental life purpose or goal that will be socially desirable and personally satisfying." In order to do this effectively, education "must start with the child as he is, with his abilities, desires, and interests, his needs and problems, his pattern of life and conduct."

These authors further state: (1) that the occupation cannot in itself furnish a satisfactory central purpose or goal; (2) that there is for most of us no one and only one position in life, occupation, or job that is predestined; (3) that one does not usually need to change his job or position in order to be useful in achieving his life purpose; and (4) that, within certain limits, one may so change the situation in which he is placed (his job) as to increase its effectiveness as an agent or element that contributes to the attainment of one's life purpose.

---

[1] Guidance in Educational Institutions, Thirty-seventh Yearbook, pt. I, p. 3. National Society for the Study of Education. Bloomington, Ill., Public-School Publishing Co., 1938.

While careful choice of a job is of great importance, there is some opportunity in most positions for such personal adjustment as will make possible the use of the occupation or other activity in the attainment of the central purpose. The oft-quoted advice, "If we spent more time in trying to like the things we have to do instead of in attempting to find the things we like, we would be happier and more effective," has some value in cases where it is impossible to secure the best job or to change the conditions in the job.

It is generally agreed that the specific functions of vocational guidance should be the following: (1) to assist the individual to choose an occupation; (2) to prepare for it; (3) to enter upon it; and (4) to make progress in it. This will require: (1) study of the individual; (2) study of the occupation; (3) counseling; (4) placement; and (5) follow-up.

The carrying out of the functions outlined above, based on the viewpoint suggested in the preceding section requires a staff, activities, and services. Many organization plans have been suggested for conducting an effective guidance program. The most recent is that proposed by the Committee on Guidance of the National Society for the Study of Education.[2] It revolves around three persons: The teacher, the guidance leader, the specialist. The role of the teacher in the guidance program will vary with the size of school and other conditions. Because of his intimate contact with the pupil he is in a strategic position to assist in personally guiding the pupil and in furnishing essential information to others interested in his proper guidance. In addition to the teacher-counselor, it is desirable to have a guidance leader in the school, someone to coordinate the efforts of the teacher and different activities and services and to see that all the potential guidance facilities of the school and community are focused on the problems of the pupil. This may be one of the teachers or the principal—in a small school; a person designated as adviser, counselor, dean, director, or personnel worker. The physician, employment expert, psychologist, social worker, and many other specialists may have a definite place in an effective guidance program. It is the business of the teacher and the guidance leader to bring the knowledge and skill of these specialists to bear on the guidance problems which pupils face. The manner of doing this naturally will vary with the community and the school. Since only a few institutions can institute a comprehensive guidance program, it is suggested that each begin with what it has, and expand as conditions permit.

Needs in schools for Negroes.—The first need in respect to guidance for Negroes is to increase the number of schools which provide a guidance program. Second, to increase the number of teachers and special guidance workers who are trained in the principles and techniques of guidance. Third, to improve the service now given so as to include such information about pupils and adults as was discussed in the two previous chapters.

---

[2] Ibid., p. 267.

Fourth, to assist all who are concerned with the education and welfare of Negroes to recognize their special needs and problems in relation to the entire educational situation.

In making effective occupational adjustments Negroes, in common with people in general, need guidance in the selection of an occupation and efficient preparation for it when chosen. An effective school program should meet both general and special problems in guidance and in vocational preparation. Many of the same problems are common to all youth. A special problem in occupational adjustment for Negroes is due to restricted employment opportunities because of racial attitudes and prejudices. The school program can contribute to the solution of this problem through offering effective guidance; by familiarizing pupils with the facts of the situation; by providing effective training for as many vocations as are open to Negroes; and by gradually widening, as the interests of students and the employment situation warrant, opportunities for training for an increasing variety of occupations.

Guidance programs should provide also for the following studies of occupations: (1) the total number and the number of Negroes now engaged in each; (2) the increase and decrease of both the total number and of Negroes in numbers and percents; (3) the probable future demand for workers; and (4) the number preparing for each of the occupations. Negro youth should be given the facts regarding racial difficulties; the prevailing economic conditions; and causes so far as they are known of the present occupational situation with suggested remedies. They should be helped to realize that no single remedy will solve their problems. Individual capacity, initiative, and character will always be essential in effective participation in the changing economic world.

APPENDIX A

Additional Statistical Data

TABLE I.—*Number of Negro students and percent of all students enrolled in federally aided vocational courses, by years and States*

State	1928–29		1929–30		1930–31		1931–32		1932–33		1933–34		1934–35	
	Number	Percent	Number	Percent	Number	Percent	Number	Percent	Number	Percent	Number	Percent	Number	Percent
1	2	3	4	5	6	7	8	9	10	11	12	13	14	15
	MALES													
Alabama	1,401	14.1	1,488	14.3	1,941	14.4	2,591	17.2	2,412	19.3	1,920	17.3	2,685	18.1
Arkansas	1,937	28.4	2,463	27.8	2,711	22.6	2,749	55.6	2,633	28.2	2,800	26.4	2,526	20.1
Delaware	33	2.2	40	2.5	32	2.8	57	5.1	35	2.8	17	1.3	65	3.5
Florida	385	9.8	535	12.8	604	12.8	981	14.2	1,684	24.6	1,190	19.0	1,445	18.0
Georgia	2,679	25.3	2,555	19.6	3,306	20.9	3,142	16.2	3,414	20.0	2,497	12.5	3,464	12.7
Kentucky	136	3.2	133	2.0	170	2.5	190	2.9	200	2.7	281	3.6	91	1.1
Louisiana	2,085	27.9	1,270	19.0	1,360	16.9	2,116	22.6	2,916	23.8	3,427	35.4	4,412	39.0
Maryland	263	8.2	213	6.2	290	8.9	362	8.6	329	7.1	565	12.9	899	18.8
Mississippi	1,994	28.5	2,120	20.1	3,651	34.3	3,621	23.6	3,753	24.1	4,714	25.2	6,220	29.1
Missouri	560	5.6	243	1.6	210	1.7	423	4.1	309	2.7	343	2.9	448	3.8
New Jersey	45	0.3	175	0.9	266	1.3	226	1.2	237	1.5	228	1.6	207	1.1
North Carolina	1,936	13.1	2,042	13.5	2,132	13.3	2,904	17.0	3,037	17.4	3,063	14.9	3,450	14.2
Oklahoma	655	8.8	708	7.3	862	7.0	3,151	23.8	874	9.7	1,042	6.5	1,350	9.7
South Carolina	2,647	18.0	3,092	17.8	3,547	17.2	4,431	24.1	3,757	19.8	4,869	19.9	4,531	18.2
Tennessee	896	12.3	1,165	9.2	2,105	13.3	2,071	12.5	2,134	13.8	1,770	10.5	2,060	10.4
Texas	2,278	15.1	1,791	14.1	3,208	15.5	4,108	19.4	464	8.6	6,005	18.8	7,288	17.6
Virginia	1,996	20.0	2,143	17.0	3,176	17.6	2,270	14.2	2,581	13.0	2,493	15.8	3,099	17.8
West Virginia	79	2.8	80	2.7	90	2.6	115	2.8	144	4.2	173	4.5	116	2.1
Total	22,005	------	22,256	1.1	29,661	34.8	35,508	61.4	30,913	40.5	37,397	69.9	44,356	101.6
Grand total	157,269	------	184,229	17.1	215,213	36.8	224,955	43.0	203,036	29.1	246,041	56.4	288,942	83.7

TABLE I.—*Number of Negro students and percent of all students enrolled in federally aided vocational courses, by years and States*—Continued

State	1928-29		1929-30		1930-31		1931-32		1932-33		1933-34		1934-35	
	Number	Percent	Number	Percent	Number	Percent	Number	Percent	Number	Percent	Number	Percent	Number	Percent
1	2	3	4	5	6	7	8	9	10	11	12	13	14	15
FEMALES														
Alabama	75	6.3	717	30.9	923	25.2	1,526	25.9	2,127	22.4	1,719	31.3	2,388	18.9
Arkansas	621	35.8	150	7.6	826	22.7	848	14.0	878	16.1	934	17.6	1,195	16.5
Delaware	64	10.1	30	5.4	25	5.2	30	6.1	57	6.6	69	9.4	167	10.3
Florida	223	3.7	309	15.7	396	10.5	935	16.2	1,353	23.1	1,503	18.7	2,849	30.2
Georgia	1,942	30.7	1,887	17.4	1,759	17.5	1,701	15.4	2,274	15.1	2,121	15.9	1,950	13.6
Kentucky	33	1.4	169	9.8	234	8.3	140	4.9	204	6.5	117	3.8	202	5.1
Louisiana	1,129	30.7	1,189	23.5	1,302	22.1	1,718	21.7	2,020	27.9	2,086	48.4	2,163	22.5
Maryland	52	1.9	414	18.1	580	18.0	699	24.0	786	30.0	849	32.5	947	38.1
Mississippi	269	19.9	499	10.4	597	18.0	1,347	28.2	1,636	27.4	1,955	33.5	2,209	25.9
Missouri	807	9.2	664	6.4	536	6.8	858	10.0	917	12.9	423	6.2	674	7.9
New Jersey	162	9.2	181	6.1	200	1.7	216	2.0	202	2.3	471	2.8	161	2.5
North Carolina	1,117	17.5	1,146	22.6	1,281	18.5	1,624	16.4	2,069	18.6	1,878	19.5	3,683	24.8
Oklahoma	1,584	27.5	669	17.7	2,066	16.5	2,598	16.3	2,943	17.4	1,374	9.0	2,218	11.3
South Carolina	274	19.9	405	17.5	979	20.4	374	7.2	204	3.4	351	5.6	132	13.9
Tennessee	433	18.6	872	14.2	1,101	15.9	1,178	11.0	1,449	10.8	1,228	10.9	1,713	14.7
Texas	948	15.4	908	9.4	2,254	28.2	3,241	22.6	3,411	15.4	7,865	18.2	6,773	13.8
Virginia	1,292	40.7	1,258	31.3	1,183	15.0	949	18.8	897	17.7	808	19.4	1,216	19.2
West Virginia	97	8.0	103	8.8	171	12.7	212	11.6	182	9.8	65	3.4	141	5.5
Total	11,122	------	11,270	1.3	16,413	47.6	20,194	81.6	23,609	112.3	25,516	129.4	31,781	185.7
Grand total	73,068	------	90,093	23.3	108,578	48.6	129,922	77.8	147,648	102.1	156,857	114.7	197,208	169.9

TABLE II.—*Number of courses for Negroes and percent of all courses in federally aided vocational schools, by years and States*

State	1928-29		1929-30		1930-31		1931-32		1932-33		1933-34		1934-35	
	Number	Percent	Number	Percent	Number	Percent	Number	Percent	Number	Percent	Number	Percent	Number	Percent
1	2	3	4	5	6	7	8	9	10	11	12	13	14	15
Alabama	47	12.7	58	16.1	84	17.4	144	33.4	125	23.4	90	22.4	160	23.2
Arkansas	87	29.4	76	26.9	92	22.9	87	18.9	86	25.4	36	11.5	45	13.1
Delaware	2	4.0	4	9.5	3	8.1	4	25.0	3	9.1	3	7.3	4	7.4
Florida	13	5.6	25	15.0	26	10.6	81	26.0	53	17.4	63	22.7	114	41.3
Georgia	87	21.6	124	22.3	165	30.2	172	22.8	172	29.6	132	22.0	151	21.4
Kentucky	1	.9	2	.9	2	1.4	3	1.0	3	1.9	2	1.4	1	1.2
Louisiana	54	35.8	24	14.3	47	28.2	97	34.0	34	9.3	36	16.9	30	14.4
Maryland	9	9.0	5	4.7	9	11.5	8	8.3	7	8.1	11	12.4	11	11.4
Mississippi	63	22.8	87	21.9	135	22.0	152	27.4	145	29.9	159	24.5	246	29.9
Missouri	28	17.1	16	6.6	14	5.1	24	7.5	9	4.3	8	4.7	16	7.6
North Carolina	76	13.2	87	13.6	120	15.9	158	18.6	174	17.2	170	18.3	290	23.8
Oklahoma	62	21.1	55	18.7	90	20.7	91	21.6	108	23.4	70	15.0	89	18.2
South Carolina	117	23.8	155	27.2	50	8.9	174	26.0	200	28.4	194	31.6	266	29.5
Tennessee	30	9.8	58	12.9	80	14.3	81	14.2	84	14.5	68	15.9	77	11.3
Texas	81	12.5	122	15.0	201	21.1	291	22.0	203	20.8	478	22.8	430	20.1
Virginia	35	11.1	67	17.6	88	19.1	66	12.6	98	18.5	90	23.6	113	20.7
West Virginia	11	15.5	10	11.1	12	9.5	17	11.9	14	11.5	5	5.7	7	5.5
Total	803	--------	978	21.8	1,218	51.7	1,650	93.0	1,518	89.0	1,615	101.1	2,050	155.3
Grand total	5,325	--------	6,159	15.7	7,341	37.8	8,417	58.1	7,815	46.8	8,203	54.0	10,289	93.4

TABLE III.—*Number of Negro teachers and percent they are of all teachers in federally aided vocational schools, by years and States*

State	1928-29		1929-30		1930-31		1931-32		1932-33		1933-34		1934-35	
	Number	Percent	Number	Percent	Number	Percent	Number	Percent	Number	Percent	Number	Percent	Number	Percent
	2	3	4	5	6	7	8	9	10	11	12	13	14	15
Alabama	87	15.4	103	18.8	125	16.1	181	21.3	175	21.7	156	23.5	205	20.3
Arkansas	42	25.3	115	29.6	127	32.4	114	27.9	114	32.9	107	26.2	127	26.9
Delaware	4	5.0	4	14.3	3	5.2	5	4.7	4	5.1	5	5.1	11	9.4
Florida	25	10.5	36	26.1	42	15.6	73	21.9	107	26.0	79	23.1	105	23.4
Georgia	164	26.6	173		190	25.8	110	20.6	195	27.4	145	20.3	206	22.4
Kentucky	5	2.4	13	4.3	15	4.3	14	5.0	13	3.5		5.2	10	2.5
Louisiana	101	29.4	84	20.2	85	21.9	99	20.9	194	33.1	183	32.5	232	35.0
Maryland	10	4.8	21	9.3	30	13.3	35	12.0	38	28.4	42	16.3	46	19.1
Mississippi	119	24.3	129	24.3	165	24.1	208	27.2	219	28.2	234	29.4	308	31.2
Missouri	44	7.9	31		32	4.8	44	6.7	33	5.6	28	5.1	39	6.3
New Jersey	9	1.0	9	1.3	9	1.3	13	1.4	13	1.0	13	2.2	12	6.9
North Carolina	113	16.4	126	16.9	155	22.2	150⅓	16.9	173	19.0	172	19.2	227	19.5
Oklahoma	95	21.6	56	10.5	87	14.6	106	19.1	57	15.3	38	7.2	82	14.9
South Carolina	168	23.6	204	28.0	236	28.5	230⅓	30.7	227	26.6	243	23.2	292	25.3
Tennessee	47	11.9	64	12.6	88	14.3	104	16.3	109	17.5	92	17.5	115	15.4
Texas	152½	6.9	199	18.6	235	19.0	293	21.9	114	17.6	442	24.8	453	21.3
Virginia	68	21.9	74	21.2	124	20.9	113	21.7	75	13.1	73	19.0	78	15.1
West Virginia	12	8.6	13	8.2	10	6.3	13	7.2	9	5.0	6	3.3	7	2.7
Total [1]	1,265¾		1,454	14.8	1,761	39.1	1,906	50.6	1,870	47.8	2,072	63.7	2,555	101.8
Grand total [1]	7,888½		8,984	13.9	10,234	29.7	10,465	32.7	9,810	24.4	10,623	34.7	13,060	65.5

[1] Percents in total columns indicate increases over 1928-29.

TABLE IV.—*Amount and percent of Federal funds expended for vocational work, by race, years, and States*

State	1928-29 Amount	1928-29 Percent	1929-30 Amount	1929-30 Percent	1930-31 Amount	1930-31 Percent	1931-32 Amount	1931-32 Percent	1932-33 Amount	1932-33 Percent	1933-34 Amount	1933-34 Percent	1934-35 Amount	1934-35 Percent
1	2	3	4	5	6	7	8	9	10	11	12	13	14	15
Alabama:														
White	$125,890.84	88.3	$137,227.41	85.9	$157,557.64	86.7	$188,130.69	88.2	$148,594.43	86.1	$116,213.67	93.8	$186,731.00	87.0
Negro	16,724.94	11.7	22,515.99	14.1	24,218.87	13.3	25,250.65	11.8	23,892.24	13.9	7,701.61	6.2	27,831.24	13.0
Arkansas:														
White	90,811.84	83.1	105,778.19	82.6	125,961.36	84.5	126,641.40	80.1	124,976.28	84.4	114,883.06	85.7	151,679.00	84.8
Negro	18,397.66	16.9	22,331.00	17.4	22,970.75	15.4	31,478.71	19.9	23,014.34	15.6	19,223.71	14.3	27,104.74	15.2
Delaware:														
White	22,883.72	97.9	24,202.27	99.3	25,017.83	99.3	27,877.44	99.3	25,525.04	99.1	24,481.97	98.7	37,945.37	94.8
Negro	500.00	2.1	174.50	.7	165.00	.7	199.50	.7	225.00	.9	329.34	1.3	2,078.91	5.2
Florida:														
White	57,639.54	91.8	52,955.14	88.3	59,895.62	88.0	78,033.22	84.0	71,007.95	85.9	64,862.30	84.9	99,089.34	88.5
Negro	5,136.93	8.2	7,037.75	11.7	8,135.37	12.0	14,845.99	16.0	11,664.50	14.1	11,458.15	15.1	12,868.39	11.5
Georgia:														
White	144,280.59	80.7	165,553.80	82.1	182,273.96	82.0	207,604.65	85.2	169,160.56	85.4	155,008.21	87.8	223,395.32	87.4
Negro	34,492.23	19.3	36,091.52	17.9	39,960.92	18.0	36,002.96	14.8	28,968.97	14.6	21,592.85	12.2	32,088.14	12.6
Kentucky:														
White	136,969.05	98.3	154,637.90	97.1	176,086.83	96.9	185,884.92	96.9	165,753.63	94.9	148,083.72	96.3	194,050.84	97.9
Negro	2,347.50	1.7	4,643.00	2.9	5,527.87	3.1	6,020.62	3.1	8,875.50	5.1	5,621.68	3.7	4,052.37	2.1
Louisiana:														
White	93,526.71	81.1	91,713.00	80.3	606,041.59	97.0	178,367.56	89.3	112,726.35	83.1	103,676.91	84.2	140,383.05	84.6
Negro	21,855.22	18.9	22,497.74	19.7	18,849.19	3.0	21,350.02	10.7	22,923.43	16.9	19,457.03	15.8	25,591.48	15.4
Maryland:														
White	74,224.92	99.2	76,832.84	99.7	84,923.70	98.6	89,196.53	97.9	81,694.14	97.7	73,996.11	97.8	94,610.50	97.4
Negro	592.50	.8	195.00	.3	1,178.29	1.4	1,908.66	2.1	1,902.21	2.3	1,652.04	2.2	2,554.50	2.6
Mississippi:														
White	95,112.52	86.4	110,103.97	87.6	120,650.34	85.2	1,038,623.95	97.4	131,814.58	83.3	117,821.93	83.7	158,824.37	82.6
Negro	14,960.83	13.6	15,507.70	12.4	20,985.19	14.8	27,849.74	2.6	26,421.33	16.7	22,973.26	16.3	33,489.72	17.4
Missouri:														
White	197,507.28	98.5	225,918.28	98.9	243,373.66	99.2	227,473.71	98.4	207,099.66	98.3	187,262.50	99.0	262,113.10	98.6
Negro	3,069.68	1.5	2,500.00	1.1	1,930.80	.8	3,653.42	1.6	3,553.88	1.7	1,900.00	1.0	3,642.81	1.4
New Jersey:														
White	198,920.12	98.1	202,389.85	97.8	205,745.83	97.5	219,843.19	97.8	190,996.58	97.3	180,481.16	96.8	265,481.48	97.4
Negro	3,890.30	1.9	4,458.29	2.2	5,173.87	2.5	4,922.25	2.2	5,350.56	2.7	5,888.48	3.2	7,112.52	2.6
North Carolina:														
White	131,021.99	87.1	150,832.06	87.9	171,586.22	88.4	196,447.11	89.4	198,086.52	89.3	173,305.60	90.1	225,147.49	89.2
Negro	19,360.69	12.9	20,825.22	12.1	22,426.15	11.6	23,305.56	10.6	23,790.77	10.7	18,975.73	9.9	27,318.62	10.8

TABLE IV.—*Amount and percent of Federal funds expended for vocational work, by race, years, and States—Continued*

State	1928–29 Amount	Percent	1929–30 Amount	Percent	1930–31 Amount	Percent	1931–32 Amount	Percent	1932–33 Amount	Percent	1933–34 Amount	Percent	1934–35 Amount	Percent
1	2	3	4	5	6	7	8	9	10	11	12	13	14	15
Oklahoma:														
White	119,654.78	91.5	133,705.68	93.6	144,550.92	95.8	165,715.92	91.1	135,854.25	89.9	131,265.13	91.7	170,959.89	90.3
Negro	11,076.25	8.5	9,170.59	6.4	6,315.13	4.2	16,210.86	8.9	15,184.08	10.1	11,901.58	8.3	18,409.17	9.7
South Carolina:														
White	91,077.04	87.7	103,773.02	89.3	117,466.22	89.6	66,981.20	84.2	119,322.99	92.6	110,776.10	91.9	148,946.70	90.5
Negro	12,796.00	12.3	12,416.73	10.7	13,636.59	10.4	12,598.00	15.8	9,593.10	7.4	9,741.66	8.1	15,672.65	9.5
Tennessee:														
White	134,859.41	92.6	144,569.83	89.2	151,899.38	88.9	174,596.57	89.4	165,886.28	92.7	147,343.74	91.1	203,545.48	91.5
Negro	10,765.68	7.4	17,437.81	10.8	18,884.13	11.1	20,283.93	10.6	12,966.16	7.3	14,386.03	8.9	18,974.33	8.5
Texas:														
White	257,556.20	89.2	292,456.51	90.6	290,791.85	87.7	346,324.00	87.7	139,149.21	89.2	199,544.51	77.8	434,066.36	86.6
Negro	30,998.09	10.8	30,488.76	9.4	40,658.97	12.3	48,675.79	12.3	16,839.95	10.8	56,797.74	22.2	67,090.86	13.4
Virginia:														
White	121,099.26	84.1	129,390.73	83.7	123,641.97	83.7	155,116.79	85.2	146,324.36	86.9	134,666.36	87.3	187,857.23	87.8
Negro	22,966.32	15.9	25,196.10	16.3	24,144.41	16.3	26,985.50	14.8	21,974.68	13.1	19,502.87	12.7	26,147.42	12.2
West Virginia:														
White	68,218.82	95.5	81,656.71	96.4	74,368.26	94.9	94,646.62	95.4	85,328.79	95.3	66,061.71	95.3	94,514.03	97.0
Negro	3,175.43	4.5	3,027.98	3.6	3,968.41	5.1	4,519.96	4.6	4,245.00	4.7	3,240.00	4.7	2,906.42	3.0
Total:[1]														
White	2,161,254.63	90.3	2,383,697.19	10.3	3,061,833.18	41.7	3,767,505.47	74.3	2,419,301.60	11.9	2,249,734.69	4.1	3,279,340.55	51.7
Negro	233,106.25	9.7	256,515.68	10.0	279,129.71	19.7	326,062.12	39.9	261,385.70	4.1	252,343.81	8.3	354,934.29	52.3
Grand total[1]	2,394,360.88		2,640,212.87	10.3	3,340,962.89	39.5	4,093,567.59	70.9	2,680,687.30	11.9	2,502,078.50	4.5	3,634,274.84	51.8

[1] Percents in total columns from 1929–30 to 1934–35 indicate increases over 1928–29.

Table V.—Age-grade distribution of Negro high-school pupils in 33 States and the District of Columbia, according to geographical region

Age	Grade 8 Male	Grade 8 Female	Grade 8 Total	Grade 9 Male	Grade 9 Female	Grade 9 Total	Grade 10 Male	Grade 10 Female	Grade 10 Total	Grade 11 Male	Grade 11 Female	Grade 11 Total	Grade 12 Male	Grade 12 Female	Grade 12 Total	Grand total Male	Grand total Female	Grand total Total
1	2	3	4	5	6	7	8	9	10	11	12	13	14	15	16	17	18	19
SOUTH ATLANTIC REGION[1]																		
14 years or less	275	388	663	292	572	864	87	196	283	24	56	80	6	1	7	684	1,213	1,897
15	129	192	321	206	364	570	196	350	546	74	136	210	27	12	39	632	1,054	1,686
16	81	96	177	136	211	347	176	305	481	137	267	404	47	80	127	577	959	1,536
17	48	39	87	76	89	165	111	144	255	122	209	331	52	130	182	409	611	1,020
18	18	12	30	29	44	73	58	70	128	89	118	207	52	73	125	246	317	563
19	3	3	6	14	11	25	26	22	48	53	60	113	34	34	68	130	130	260
20	5	----	5	4	2	6	7	2	9	24	17	41	9	11	20	49	32	81
21	1	----	----	2	1	2	6	2	8	10	10	20	3	6	9	22	19	41
22	----	1	1	2	----	2	----	----	----	4	4	11	2	3	5	8	10	18
23	----	----	----	2	----	2	1	3	4	8	----	11	----	----	----	11	8	19
24 years or more	----	----	----	2	1	2	4	1	5	5	4	9	4	2	6	15	7	22
Total	560	731	1,291	765	1,294	2,059	672	1,095	1,767	550	888	1,438	236	352	588	2,783	4,360	7,143
Percent	20.1	16.8	18.1	27.5	29.7	28.8	24.1	25.1	24.7	19.8	20.4	20.1	8.5	8.1	8.2	100.0	100.0	100.0
Normal	275	388	663	498	936	1,434	372	655	1,027	259	476	735	104	203	307	1,508	2,658	4,166
Percent	49.1	53.1	51.4	65.1	72.3	69.6	55.4	59.8	58.1	47.1	53.6	51.1	44.1	57.7	52.2	54.2	60.9	58.3
Overage	285	343	628	267	358	625	213	244	457	193	220	413	52	56	108	1010	1,221	2,231
Percent	50.9	46.9	48.6	34.9	27.7	30.4	31.7	22.3	25.9	35.1	24.8	28.7	22.0	15.9	18.4	36.3	28.0	31.2
Underage	----	----	----	----	----	----	87	196	283	98	192	290	80	93	173	265	481	746
Percent	----	----	----	----	----	----	12.9	17.9	16.0	17.8	21.6	20.2	33.9	26.4	29.4	9.5	11.0	10.4

[1] South Atlantic region: Delaware, District of Columbia, Maryland, Kentucky, North Carolina, South Carolina, Virginia, and West Virginia.

TABLE V.—*Age-grade distribution of Negro high-school pupils in 33 States and the District of Columbia, according to geographical region*—Continued

Age	Grade 8			Grade 9			Grade 10			Grade 11			Grade 12			Grand total		
	Male	Female	Total	Male	Female	Total	Male	Female	Total	Male	Female	Total	Male	Female	Total	Male	Female	Total
	2	3	4	5	6	7	8	9	10	11	12	13	14	15	16	17	18	19
SOUTH CENTRAL REGION																		
14 years or less	70	134	204	161	327	488	50	112	162	13	30	43	1	4	5	295	607	902
15	35	45	80	142	237	379	103	185	288	50	126	176	8	22	30	338	615	953
16	20	29	49	99	154	253	104	206	310	112	192	304	36	72	108	371	653	1,024
17	9	14	23	51	76	127	84	118	202	87	165	252	65	155	220	296	528	824
18	1	—	1	25	33	58	38	61	99	60	98	158	61	128	189	185	320	505
19	—	—	—	8	10	18	29	21	50	35	31	66	48	86	134	120	148	268
20	—	—	—	8	—	18	6	4	10	9	12	21	28	20	48	63	39	102
21	—	—	—	—	3	13	2	—	7	5	6	11	15	13	28	39	18	57
22	—	—	—	8	5	13	2	2	4	2	—	3	9	4	13	18	13	31
23	—	—	—	2	1	—	1	1	4	1	1	3	3	3	6	6	6	15
24 years or more	—	—	—	3	4	6	3	3	6	—	1	2	5	4	9	12	11	23
Total	135	222	357	509	853	1,362	427	713	1,140	393	662	1,055	279	511	790	1,743	2,961	4,704
Percent	7.7	7.5	7.6	29.2	28.8	28.9	24.5	24.1	24.2	22.5	22.4	22.4	16.0	17.3	16.8	100.0	100.0	100.0
Normal	70	134	204	303	564	867	207	391	598	199	357	556	126	283	409	905	1,729	2,634
Percent	51.8	60.4	57.1	59.5	66.1	63.6	48.5	54.8	52.5	50.6	53.9	52.7	45.2	55.4	51.8	51.9	58.4	55.9
Overage	65	88	153	206	289	495	170	210	380	131	149	280	108	130	238	680	866	1,546
Percent	48.1	39.6	42.9	40.5	33.9	36.3	39.8	29.5	33.3	33.3	22.5	26.5	38.7	25.4	30.1	39.0	29.2	32.9
Underage	—	—	—	—	—	—	50	112	162	63	156	219	45	98	143	158	366	524
Percent	—	—	—	—	—	—	11.7	15.7	14.2	16.0	23.6	20.8	16.1	19.2	18.1	9.1	12.4	11.1
SOUTHWEST REGION																		
14 years or less	177	260	437	142	260	402	26	87	113	15	20	35	—	5	5	360	632	992
15	75	124	199	157	298	455	102	192	294	38	90	128	3	12	15	375	716	1,091
16	50	95	145	134	203	337	131	237	368	75	216	291	20	41	61	410	792	1,202
17	31	44	75	92	85	177	96	151	247	106	217	323	31	64	95	356	561	917
18	20	15	35	39	45	84	55	75	130	94	152	246	43	49	92	251	336	587
19	3	3	6	12	18	30	25	18	43	68	66	134	24	29	53	132	134	266
20	1	2	3	8	3	11	17	6	23	24	23	47	19	17	36	69	51	120

	C1	C2	C3	C4	C5	C6	C7	C8	C9	C10	C11	C12	C13	C14	C15	C16	C17	C18
21	1					1	2	1	3	7	12	19	12	5	17	23	18	41
22			1		2	2	2		2	4	2	6	2	2	4	8	6	14
23				1						2	3	5	2	1	3	4	4	8
24 years or more		1					2		2				2	1	3	5	1	6
Total	358	544	902	585	914	1,499	458	767	1,225	433	801	1,234	159	225	384	1,993	3,251	5,244
Percent	18.0	16.7	17.2	29.3	28.1	28.6	22.9	23.6	23.4	21.7	24.6	23.5	7.9	6.9	7.3	100.0	100.0	100.0
Normal	177	260	437	299	558	857	233	429	662	181	433	614	74	113	187	964	1,793	2,757
Percent	49.3	47.8	48.4	51.2	61.1	57.2	50.9	55.9	54.0	41.8	54.1	49.8	46.5	50.2	48.7	48.4	55.2	52.6
Overage	181	284	465	286	356	642	199	251	450	199	258	457	62	54	116	927	1,203	2,130
Percent	50.4	52.2	51.6	48.9	38.9	42.8	43.4	32.7	36.7	45.9	32.2	37.0	38.9	24.0	30.2	46.5	37.0	40.6
Underage							26	87	113	53	110	163	23	58	81	102	255	357
Percent							5.7	11.3	9.2	12.2	13.7	13.2	14.5	25.8	21.1	5.1	7.8	6.8

NORTHERN REGION[4]

	N1	N2	N3	N4	N5	N6	N7	N8	N9	N10	N11	N12	N13	N14	N15	N16	N17	N18
14 years or less	17	33	50	430	682	1,112	95	182	277	13	9	22	3	2	5	558	908	1,466
15	9	15	24	503	683	1,186	334	559	893	83	175	258	21	18	39	950	1,450	2,400
16	5	9	14	390	378	768	401	593	994	236	461	697	56	133	189	1,088	1,574	2,662
17	2	2	4	160	121	281	243	271	514	257	426	683	160	293	453	822	1,113	1,935
18	20	2	22	44	24	68	93	110	203	167	290	457	177	259	436	501	685	1,186
19	14		14	20		21	24	23	47	60	69	129	136	110	246	254	203	457
20	3		3	4		4	4	3	7	15	16	31	41	31	72	67	50	117
21							1	2	3	1	2	5	17	11	23	17	15	32
22							1		1	1	2	3	1		7	9	2	11
23						1			1						1	3		3
24 years or more				1		1					1	1	1	2		2	4	6
Total	70	61	131	1,553	1,889	3,442	1,197	1,744	2,941	836	1,451	2,287	615	859	1,474	4,271	6,004	10,275
Percent	1.6	1.0	1.3	36.4	31.5	33.5	28.0	29.0	28.6	19.6	24.2	22.3	14.4	14.3	14.3	100.0	100.0	100.0
Normal	17	33	50	933	1,365	2,298	735	1,152	1,887	493	887	1,380	337	552	889	2,515	3,989	6,504
Percent	24.3	54.1	38.2	60.1	72.3	66.8	61.4	66.1	64.2	58.9	61.1	60.3	54.8	64.3	60.3	58.9	66.4	63.3
Overage	53	28	81	620	524	1,144	367	410	777	247	380	627	198	154	352	1,485	1,496	2,981
Percent	75.7	45.9	61.8	39.9	27.7	33.2	30.7	23.5	26.4	29.5	26.2	27.4	32.2	17.9	23.9	34.8	24.9	29.0
Underage							95	182	277	96	184	280	80	153	233	271	519	790
Percent							7.9	10.4	9.4	11.5	12.7	12.2	13.0	17.8	15.8	6.3	8.6	7.7

3 South Central region: Alabama, Florida, Georgia, Mississippi, and Tennessee.
3 Southwest region: Arkansas, Kansas, Louisiana, Missouri, Oklahoma, Texas.
4 Northern region: California, Connecticut, Colorado, Illinois, Indiana, Iowa, Massachusetts, Michigan, New Jersey, New York, Ohio, Pennsylvania, Washington, Wisconsin.

TABLE VI.—*Grade level attained by non-graduates, according to size of community*

Grade level attained	Fewer than 2,500		2,500 to 24,999		25,000 to 99,999		100,000 to 499,999		500,000 and more		Total	
	Male	Female	Male	Female	Male	Female	Male	Female	Male	Female	Male	Female
1	2	3	4	5	6	7	8	9	10	11	12	13
7	2	1	6	6	2	2	12	2	27	25	49	36
8	16	19	89	112	293	392	105	110	29	22	532	655
9	80	102	145	262	274	456	435	557	126	148	1,060	1,525
10	49	85	128	230	247	410	466	645	159	273	1,049	1,643
11	26	77	78	127	99	223	349	445	145	210	697	1,082
12	7	14	19	39	23	45	151	201	49	98	249	397
No response			1	1	3	6	2	4		3	6	14
Total	180	298	466	777	941	1,534	1,520	1,964	535	779	3,642	5,352

TABLE VII.—*Number of persons who pursued given curriculums while in high school, according to size of communities in which schools were located*

Curriculum pursued	Size of community											
	Fewer than 2,500		2,500 to 24,999		25,000 to 99,999		100,000 to 499,999		500,000 and more		Total	
	Graduates	Drop	Graduates	Drop	Graduates	Drop	Graduates	Drop	Graduates	Drop	Graduates	Drop
1	2	3	4	5	6	7	8	9	10	11	12	13
MALE												
Academic	127	112	388	297	652	634	1,077	925	423	189	2,667	2,157
Trades	5	6	36	26	74	78	228	278	60	132	403	520
Industrial arts	4	1	16	28	87	97	50	77	51	70	208	273
Teacher-training	10		25	4	15	4	25	7	3	5	78	20
Agriculture	16	44	27	20	3	8	1	4		2	47	78
Home economics		1	3	1	2	8	8	5	1	6	14	21
Commercial	1		12	6	10	9	51	67	39	51	113	133
Other	11	14	70	72	88	97	123	144	70	76	362	403
No response	2	2	4	12	8	6	6	13	6	4	26	37
Total	176	180	581	466	939	941	1,569	1,520	653	535	3,918	3,642
FEMALE												
Academic	173	185	579	417	1,118	961	2,177	1,318	678	225	4,725	3,106
Trades		2	2	2	6	7	52	66	68	89	128	166
Industrial arts	3	3	1	10	39	51	48	61	22	20	113	145
Teacher-training	20	9	141	36	79	43	67	21	13	6	320	115
Agriculture	2	2	1	1	3	1		3			6	7
Home economics	53	71	180	184	362	292	185	189	124	129	904	865
Commercial	5		14	12	40	30	256	134	261	225	576	401
Other	10	24	131	106	129	142	134	157	137	78	541	507
No response	2	2	5	9	9	7	13	15	6	7	35	40
Total	268	298	1,054	777	1,785	1,534	2,932	1,964	1,309	779	7,348	5,352

TABLE VIII.—*Number of graduates and nongraduates indicating whether or not they were employed during their high-school attendance, by size of community*

Employed during high-school career	Male graduates by size of community						Male nongraduates by size of community					
	Fewer than 2,500	2,500–24,999	25,000–99,999	100,000–499,999	500,000 and more	Total	Fewer than 2,500	2,500–24,999	25,000–99,999	100,000–499,999	500,000 and more	Total
1	2	3	4	5	6	7	8	9	10	11	12	13
Yes_____	103	363	519	854	347	2,186	90	219	411	703	186	1,609
No_____	70	210	410	704	298	1,692	85	245	516	792	344	1,982
No response_____	3	8	10	11	8	40	5	2	14	25	5	51
Total_____	176	581	939	1,569	653	3,918	180	466	941	1,520	535	3,642
	Female graduates						Female nongraduates					
Yes_____	55	325	394	712	321	1,807	57	195	292	460	176	1,180
No_____	210	724	1,375	2,199	974	5,482	235	577	1,211	1,486	595	4,104
No response_____	3	5	16	21	14	59	6	5	31	18	8	68
Total_____	268	1,054	1,785	2,932	1,309	7,348	298	777	1,534	1,964	779	5,352

=======[*APPENDIX B*]=======

Organization, Personnel, and Inquiry Forms

ORGANIZATION AND STAFF

Because of the nature and scope of the survey it was necessary to centralize its administration and supervision in the Office of Education. A Director, Associate Director, and four Regional Directors devoted their entire time to its administration and supervision. The Regional Directors had offices at Richmond, Va.; Birmingham, Ala.; Houston, Tex.; and Columbus, Ohio, for regions 1, 2, 3, and 4, respectively. They supervised the initiation of the survey in each State and maintained contacts between the central office and the State staffs. In addition to the central staff, each State unit was under the direction of a Project Manager and a Supervisor. In some cases the functions of both were performed by one person. In most cases these persons were full-time employees who were loaned by school systems, colleges, and social agencies.

While the survey was a research project, it was also designed to provide work for unemployed "white collar" workers on the relief rolls. The major part of the interviewing and collecting of data for the study was done by such workers. There were approximately 500 of them. Thirty-five percent held the bachelor's degree, and 50 percent had from 1 to 4 years of college education. Twelve held the master's degree. All the nonrelief workers (supervisors and project managers) had university training, six held the doctor's degree or its equivalent.

PERSONNEL

The chief types of experience the workers had before employment in the study, and the number of persons in each type, follow:

Teaching 170
Social work 41
Tabulating and statistical work 115
Stenography and typing 85
Filing 213
Miscellaneous research work 246

Other vocations followed by three or more persons include: Ministry, medicine, law, nursing, librarianship, insurance, and recreational work. The number, education, experience, and other data concerning the relief workers are shown in the following table:

134

GENERAL CENSUS OF RELIEF PERSONNEL

1. Number of relief workers: Male, 205; female, 274; total, 479.
2. Marital status: Married, 221; single, 258.
3. Number having given educational preparation:

1. High-school education, 75	4. Graduate work, 34
2. Attended college, 227	5. Master's degree, 12
3. Bachelor's degree, 131	

4. Number having designated types of experience:

Teachers	170	Bookkeepers	3
Clerks	119	Printers	2
Secretaries	90	Editors	2
Typists	57	Farmers	2
Social workers	41	Morticians	2
Investigators	35	Correspondent	1
Stenographers	28	Photographer	1
Supervisors	20	Architect	1
Recreational directors	14	Druggist	1
Unskilled laborers	13	Proprietor	1
Skilled laborers	12	Matron	1
Librarians	7	Registrar	1
Preachers	5	Accountant	1
Project directors	4	Writer	1
Insurance agents	4	Musician	1
Nurses	4	Reporter	1
Principals	4	Dentist	1
Lawyers	4	Gardener	1
Addressographers	3	Contractor	1
Salesmen	3	Designer	1
Business managers	3	Real estate agent	1

5. Number having special qualifications:

Courses in—		Experience in—	
Tests and measurements	139	Interviewing	246
Guidance	122	Filing	213
Trades	91	Typing	139
Statistics	72	Scoring tests	133
Tabulating	44	Tabulating	115
		Shorthand	63

INQUIRY FORMS

Inquiry forms Ac and Ah were for colleges and high schools, respectively. They were for the purpose of collecting information concerning organization, administration, curriculum offerings, vocational curriculum trends, enrollment and registration trends, and use of Federal funds for vocational education. Usable returns were received from 73 colleges and 207 high schools.

Inquiry form E was for the purpose of obtaining information concerning the content and methods of teaching representative courses in vocational education and guidance in high schools. The types of information sought about the courses were: Requirements, sequences, purposes, assignments, methods, tests, and materials. There were 968 of these forms that were usable.

Inquiry form F was designed to ascertain facts concerning housing facilities and amount and kinds of equipment available for vocational courses. Although 293 of these forms were received the lack of comparable data in some cases and the inadequacy of data in other cases considerably reduced the number that were usable. (Data not included in this report.)

Inquiry forms I and J were for evening and proprietary schools and social agencies, and were designed to gather the same general information from these institutions as was obtained from colleges and high schools through Ac and Ah. Returns were received from 64 evening and proprietary schools and 70 social agencies. However, all these returns were not usable.

Form D was designed for the purpose of collecting personnel data from pupils enrolled in the last 4 years of high school. The specific objectives were to collect information concerning certain socio-economic background factors; present educational status, and educational and vocational interests and plans. Usable returns were received from 27,984 pupils.

Form G is another personnel form. It was used to collect information concerning teachers of vocational education and guidance in high schools for Negroes. Information was gathered concerning their academic, professional, and vocational training, and their teaching and trade experience. The teachers, personally, received the form from the interviewers and were assured of the confidential manner in which the data would be treated. After filling in the form each teacher returned it directly to the Office of Education in a self-addressed envelope. Data were received from 1,001 teachers.

Form H also has to do with personnel data. Its purpose was to collect facts from students in evening schools concerning course registration, previous education, job experience, and the student's opinion concerning the value of vocational courses previously taken. Returns were received from 2,540 students.

Form K was a guidance inquiry for the purpose of gathering information concerning the guidance program, personnel, and policies in certain institutions. The institutions to which form K was sent had previously been identified by the use of form X, which among other things requested institutions to indicate whether or not they had a guidance program. Although 602 institutions answered in the affirmative, only 129 high schools and 35 colleges returned form K. It is assumed that most of those that did not reply realized, after the receipt of form K, that they did not have any guidance program. This belief is strengthened by many letters expressing this view.

Form M obtained personnel information from 368 students in nurse-training institutions. Data collected on the form included previous training, reasons for vocational choice, plans for the future, and education and occupation of parents. (Data not presented in this report.)

Forms L and Z were designed to obtain personnel information concerning former pupils and graduates of high schools from 1926 to 1935, inclusive. Usable information on these forms was supplied by 20,260 persons. The major purpose of this inquiry was to ascertain the relation, if any, between the occupational status and previous schooling and background. Data were gathered concerning such items as occupation of parents, curriculum pursued, subject preference, extracurriculum participation, occupational preference and experience, vocational training, age and grade level at time of leaving school, and reason for leaving school.

Form X, a preliminary inquiry designed to identify institutions offering courses in vocational education and guidance, was sent to all secondary schools and colleges for Negroes in January 1936. The data requested concerned number and kind of curriculum offerings, number of grades or years offered, specific offerings in vocational education, extent of guidance or personnel services. Responses were received from all the colleges for Negroes, all of the 4-year and senior high schools, and many secondary schools offering 1 to 3 years of work. It was possible from this preliminary survey to select institutions for special purposes of the survey.

○